Our Bruguier Family: Descendants and Ancestors of Francis Bruguier of Newark, N.J.

Lise K. Doss
Copyright 2016

Dedication

To my husband, Curtis Doss, without whose patience and encouragement I could not have spent so much time researching, and to my daughters Navvab Taylor and Ruhi Bell, my primary audience, with much love.

Note to Reader:

This book is about the Bruguier family who lived in Germany and New Jersey. The family is not related to the wealthy Bruguier family of New York, Newport and San Francisco society pages. Nor is it related to the Bruguier family centered in South Dakota, whose roots are French and Native American.

Much of the information presented here was gathered from the US federal census, taken every decade, as well as birth, marriage and death records, both American and German, available online at www.familysearch.org and www.ancestry.com. Old newspaper articles are available online at www.genealogybank.com and www.newspapers.com. Some are available outside those databases, due to local library projects, for instance the Red Bank Register, covering Monmouth County, N.J., available at rbr.mtpl.org/rbr. Old newspapers and books can be accessed through books.google.com. There are more German resources available by using .de instead of .com in various web sites. We also were fortunate to have letters and photos sent to us in the 1960s from relatives in Germany. I found many more relatives than I had known of when I started the project, but the emphasis is on my branch of the family as those are the people I knew or knew of. In the interest of privacy I have primarily brought the family line only down to people living in the mid twentieth century.

To improve readability, I have not footnoted events in this narrative. The interested reader who wants to see more details may consult my family tree "Kirner" at www.ancestry.com, or an earlier, but free tree at http://wc.rootsweb.ancestry.com/cgi-bin/igm.cgi?op=SHOW&db=ldoss&recno=455. A report of sources used is at the end of this book.

TABLE OF CONTENTS

OUR BRUGUIER FAMILY

INTRODUCTION

I spent a lot of time with my mother's mother when I was growing up. Her name was Viola Elizabeth Bertha Bruguier. This little book is to honor her and her family.

We don't know where the family came from in France, but today the distribution of the name is all across southern France. My grandmother told me her family left France because they were Huguenots. The Huguenots were the French Protestants. They were subject to even more persecution than the Protestants in England and Germany, and the majority of Huguenots did live in southern France. Our Bruguieres fled to Germany. At that time, there was no Germany as we know it today; Germany was a collection of a couple dozen small principalities. One of the most powerful was Prussia, which, under the leadership of Frederick the Great, who ruled in the mid to late 1600s, became the dominant kingdom among the German states. In the 1685 Edict of Potsdam, Frederick actively recruited Huguenots to settle the area around Berlin. By 1700 one third of Berlin was French immigrants. This is the place we can trace our Bruguiers back to, so it is likely that they emigrated at that time.

My grandmother's Bruguier grandfather came to America in 1862 but the family corresponded with family in Germany for a couple of generations. Her older sister Alma had a few letters from German cousins written about 1960 that told her of the family history as they remembered it and as it was recorded in their family Bible. Sometimes those accounts agree with vital records of the time, sometimes they do not. The letters are reproduced in the appendices. They also sent the photos of the parents of our immigrant ancestor, their son, and his wife, which are reproduced in this book.

Generation after generation, the Bruguiers married other Germans, and spoke German at home through my grandmother's time; she did not learn English until she went to school. My mother recalls that her grandparents spoke with German accents even though they lived their whole lives in New Jersey.

Since the family was mostly German, they used a German pronunciation for their name. You can see it in newspaper advertisements from the family business around 1910, where it says "Bruguier's (pronounced: Broogeers)". Starting around WWI, sometimes her family spelled it Bruguiere. The "ier" or "iere" ending is typical of French words, but the French pronunciation is totally different. According to the way the family pronounces the name today, the name in France was probably originally written "Bruguiere". No French speaking person would have pronounced it as "Broogeers".

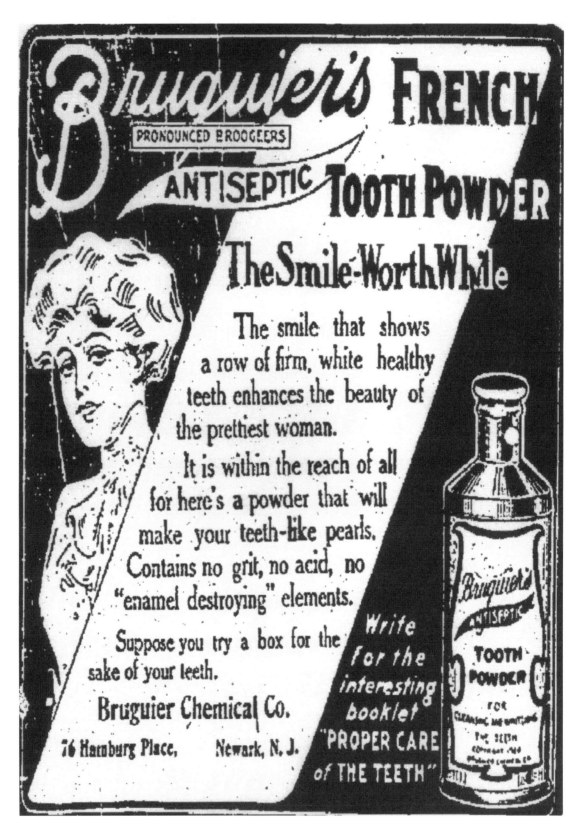

BRUGUIER CHEMICAL COMPANY ADVERTISEMENT IN JERSEY JOURNAL, JAN. 5, 1910, SHOWING THE WAY THEY PRONOUNCED THEIR NAME AT THAT TIME. THAT IS A GERMAN PRONUNCIATION. A search on Google will bring up more old advertisements.

PART ONE: BEFORE IMMIGRATION TO AMERICA
THE FIRST GENERATION WE KNOW OF

JOHANN VON BRUGUIER

According to the letters from our relatives in Germany, the oldest ancestor they remembered was Johann von Bruguier, a professional solder who was a captain in the infantry, specifically the Regiment von Stain of the Austrian Army of Italy. They said he died in battle in or near Milan, Italy on August 20, 1794. There seems to be a little confusion here. The Regiment von Stain was from Württemberg, not Austria, and there was no battle in Milan at that time.

THE SECOND GENERATION

CARL JOSEPH VON BRUGUIER AND ALBERTINE KAROLINE HENRIETTA NEGENDANK

The only child of Johann's of whom we have any record was his son Carl Joseph von Bruguier. Bible records (of which we have no copy, just the letters) showed his birth as April 29, 1786. Like his father, he was a career military man, being a first lieutenant in the Prussian Army, attached to Regiment 35 Corps 6 20 that was garrisoned in Potsdam, Spandau and Nauen. We don't have a marriage record, but the letter said he married in Berlin, and there are baptisms of children listed at www.familysearch.org that show his wife was variously named Henrietta Albertine Negendank, or Albertine Karoline Henriette Negendank. There are records of the baptisms of five children born to them in Jülich, today a small town about 33 miles west of Cologne, near today's border of Belgium and Germany. In 1814 Jülich changed hands from the French to the Prussians as a result of the defeat of Napoleon, and likely is why Carl Joseph von Bruguier was stationed there. Also, there was no country called Germany at that time. There was a German confederation of about three dozen German-speaking nation states, of which the most powerful was Prussia.

Our ancestor Carl Friedrich Alexander von Bruguier was born in Jülich on October 29, 1814. Perhaps Carl Joseph was then stationed elsewhere, or the family suffered the loss of other children, but there is a 12 year gap until the birth records of any other children born to them (available online at least). Then there are baptism records for four more children born to Carl Joseph and Henrietta Albertine, from 1826 to 1833. We know they had the same mother as C.F. Alexander because she is named in the records. The first was Hugo Andreas Carl von Bruguier, born Nov. 11, 1826 in Jülich, baptized the next day. The second was Berta Maria Christina von Bruguier, born in the same town on August 20, 1828, and baptized the next day. The third was Otto Ludwig Friedrich Arnold Carl von Bruguier, born the same town on March 15, 1831 and baptized the next day. And the fourth was Carl Emil Wilhelm Georg von Bruguier, baptized in the same town on July 16, 1833. Berta and Alexander are the only children mentioned in the letters from Alexander's grandchildren; perhaps the other children died in infancy.

It was common at that time for German speakers to have multiple first and middle names. Often the first name was not used, and they went by one of the middle names for every day usage. This also seems to be class related. Children of farmers often had only one or two first names, but children of higher ranking men would have three or four or more names before their surname.

Evidently Carl Joseph's military service came to an end and he returned home to the Berlin area. The letters say Albertine Henrietta died on December 10, 1844 in Charlottenburg, a small town then that is today a neighborhood of downtown Berlin. There is a listing on the Prussian state archives web site that confirms this death date and her maiden name (it is for a probate record). It refers to her as the wife of a first lieutenant, so the family letters calling him a captain were a bit of an exaggeration. The letters said her husband died a year later, on December 28, 1845 in Potsdam, a town about 20 miles southwest of Berlin. (Would his wife's estate have been probated if he were still alive? Probably he died before she did).

THE THIRD GENERATION

CARL FRIEDRICH ALEXANDER VON BRUGUIER AND SOPHIE HENRIETTE HERMINE KLEINHOLZ

Our ancestor Carl Friedrich Alexander von Bruguier was born in Jülich, on October 29, 1814. In some records his name is spelled Carl, in others it is spelled Karl. As an adult he went into the civil service. In 1840 he married Sophie Henriette Hermine Kleinholz, born in Altdöbern, Oberspreewald-Lausitz, in Brandenburg, on July 28, 1819. Altdöbern is today a tiny village roughly halfway between Berlin and Dresden. Brandenburg was a province that was the heart of the Kingdom of Prussia. Alexander and Hermine's first child was Carl Ernst August Franz, born in Seeburg, a village just west of Berlin, now part of Dallgow-Doeberitz, on May 23, 1841. He became Francis Bruguier in America in the 1860s. In April 1842 a newspaper in Potsdam ran an advertisement for the sale of Mr. von Bruguier's house with acres of woods and meadow. They may have moved to or near Senftenberg since the family letters thought that was where their children were born. Senftenburg was a military post a little south of Pritzen and Altdöbern. I was fortunate to spend almost a year at Dresden, and learned a lot of German. I contacted the minister at the church in Senftenberg, and he replied they had no records of Bruguier births at Senftenberg. Bertha Louise Agnes Emma von Bruguier was born May 14, 1843 in Pritzen, Calau, Brandenburg, according to the baptism record available at www.familysearch.org. Pritzen is a tiny place just across a small lake from Altdöbern, and not far from Senftenberg. Perhaps Hermine went home to her parents for help with the second child. The new baby went by Emma and was baptized in the Lutheran church at Pritzen on June 18, 1843. Emma grew up to marry Wilhelm Arlt, and it was her children and grandchildren who wrote of the Bible records to our family. The third child was Friedrich Otto Eugen Rudolph von Bruguier, born May 14, 1844, possibly in Senftenburg. The fourth child was Paul Bruguier, born September 22, 1845, who died in infancy. The fifth was Richard Bruguier, birth date unknown, but who died in 1856, and the last was Friedrich Wilhelm Julius Otto von Bruguier, born July 23, 1857.

Carl Friedrich Alexander worked as a Kanzler (Chancellor, a government official) in Landsberg an der Warthe in Neumark, Brandenburg (today Gorzów Wielkopolski in Poland). That town is another likely candidate for the birthplace of the younger children. The couple still lived there in 1890 when a newspaper article noted they celebrated their 50th wedding anniversary at a nearby spa in Bad Freienwalde during the summer. The article referred to her as Hermine. A list of family birth and death dates passed down in our family shows he died on April 8, 1894 and Hermine died on March 6, 1900. The relatives in Germany sent photos of them. The photo of Alexander could be from the early 1870s as wide ties were in style then, and he has some grey hair.

And here is Sophie Henriette Hermine Kleinholz von Bruguier:

These sleeves, with the exposed white undersleeves, were fashionable in the 1860s.

PART TWO: OUR BRUGUIERS IN AMERICA

THE FOURTH GENERATION

CARL ERNST AUGUST FRANZ VON BRUGUIER AND ANNA WILHELMINE LADEWIG

Our ancestor Carl Ernst August Franz von Bruguier was born in Seeburg, a village near Spandau, just west of Berlin, on May 23, 1841. He was the oldest child in the family. For reasons unknown, when he turned 21, he left what appeared to be a prosperous family situation and emigrated to America. He departed from Bremen on a type of sailing ship called a bark, the Coriolan, and the passenger list says he was a 24 year old merchant. He arrived in New York City on June 26, 1862 and enlisted in the US Army on June 30, in Company/Battery G, 5th Regiment, US Artillery in the middle of the American Civil War. His enlistment papers call him Francois Bruguier, a 24 year old apothecary, born in "Zebourg Sponda" (Seeburg by Spandau), blue eyes, brown hair, fair, 5 foot 10 and a half inches tall. Once he arrived in America he dropped the "Von" from his name, and went by Frank or Francis. One would suppose that if he wanted a military career he could have done that in Germany. It's possible he was short of cash; there were incidents of new arrivals being swindled with counterfeit currency exchange at the docks.

Battery/Company G of the 5th US Artillery Regiment was just being organized and equipped in June 1862 in New York. They were stationed at Ft. Hamilton in Brooklyn, N.Y. until December 1862. He was then stationed at Fort Morgan in Mobile, Alabama. Next he marched with his unit to New Orleans, and from April through June 1863 he saw heavy fighting in the siege at Port Hudson, Louisiana. That was the longest siege in American history, lasting 48 days. The operations were meant to separate the Confederacy from Texas, Arkansas and Louisiana, including the port at New Orleans. By at least October 1863 he was working as hospital steward and apothecary in the Army hospital at Port Hudson, La., as evidenced by a letter of recommendation for promotion by Asst. Surgeon R. W. Huntingon, dated Nov. 19, 1863, and included in Francis' application of Dec. 7, 1863 from New Orleans. In his application, Private Francois Bruguier applied to become a hospital steward, saying he was an experienced professional druggist and chemist. By Dec. 21, 1863 he was ordered to Fort Hamilton in New York and was promoted to hospital steward. He was ordered to the medical director Army Corps on Dec. 31, 1863. In the spring of 1864 he participated in the Red River Campaign in Louisiana. The troops were ordered to march up the Red River in Louisiana, capture Shreveport, and attack Texas from the east. They captured Alexandria, Louisiana in March, but fought several savage battles in April and May, with mixed results. He was posted to Fort Hamilton, N.Y. on Sep 19, 1864, but his regiment was at the Siege of Petersburg from Nov. 1864 to April 1865, then the Appomattox Campaign, where he was present when Robert E. Lee surrendered, ending the Civil War.

The family still has a letter of recommendation for him written by his commanding officer:

HeadQuarters 5th Corps Army of Potomac
June 27th 1865
To Whom it may concern,
During the past six months the bearer hereof Francis Bruguier, Hospital Steward U.S. Army, has served under me as Hospital Steward, and it affords me much pleasure to be able to testify to his character as a strictly temperate and sober man, and worthy of every confidence that I have reposed in him.
He is a man of first rate business qualifications, an excellent druggist and clerk.
I have met with but few his equal in the service, in point of qualification, and none more strictly temperate and reliable.
W.S.Thompson
Surgeon U.S. Vols.

After he was discharged from the 5th Army Corps on June 30, 1865, he returned to New York City and became a naturalized citizen in Brooklyn on July 10, 1865. Here is his signature:

Only a month and a half later, government officials in Brandenburg learned of this and issued a proclamation referring to him leaving the country without permission. German law banned a man from leaving the country without first completing his military service, paying debts, and applying to leave the country. The newspaper notice referred to him as Carl Ernst August von Bruguier from Baerwalde, born May 23, 1841 at Seeburg by Spandau, Lutheran. Today Baerwalde, Brandenburg is Mieszkowice, Poland. It's a little east of Bad Freienwalde, and 63 kilometers north of Frankfurt an den Oder, Germany. This notice is reproduced in the appendix.

On February 27, 1866 in New York City, he married Anna Wilhelmine Ladewig, a 19 year old girl born on Aug. 23, 1846 in Brandenburg to Edward Ladewig and Wilhelmine Rabach Ladewig. Her family had immigrated to New York in 1855. The wedding took place at the residence of the pastor of the Protestant Episcopal Congregation of St. George German Chapel, 91 2nd St. in New York City. The pastor was Dr. Charles Schram. The building was still standing in December 2003, see the photo below:

The actual church was located at E. 14th St. near First Ave. in 1859, and closed in 1878. The current parent church is the St. George Episcopal Church at 207 E. 16th, but the records have apparently been lost. The groom was listed as Mr. C. E. Francis A. Bruguier, 24 years, a merchant. The bride was 19, and the witnesses were her brother and sister Gustav Ladewig and Mary Ladewig. Anna's father was a light house keeper in Brooklyn and later in New Dorp, Staten Island, N.Y. He later worked as a "lampist" and engineer. These may have all been different descriptions of the same job.

Here is a photo of Francis wearing his Civil War uniform, holding his hat:

And here is a photo of his wife, Anna Wilhelmine Ladewig:

In 1866 their first child, Arthur Bruguier, was born. Sadly, the New-Yorker Staats-Zeitung newspaper carried a death notice for him on its Dec. 8, 1869 edition, calling him 3 and a half.

Francis started his pharmacy in Newark, New Jersey, in 1869 at 553 Market St., on the corner of Van Buren and Market St. Another son, Carl Frank E. was born in April 1870. That baby died on July 18, 1871. On April 3, 1872, Francis applied for a US passport. The physical description on it is: age 31 years, 6 feet tall, high forehead, blue eyes, aquiline nose, proportionate mouth, round chin, brown hair, healthy complexion, and oval face. Six feet tall was well above average in those days. Presumably he intended to travel back to Germany to see his family;

however, I don't see him on any online passenger lists. Probably he took the photos of his bride and himself in the Civil War uniform to his parents, and that is how Erwin Arlt came to have them to send back to us in the 1960s.

Paul Charles Bruguier was born on Oct 11, 1872, and was the first child of theirs to live to adulthood. Oscar Richard Bruguier was born on Dec. 15, 1873. In 1873 they lived at 115 Clinton Ave. in Newark. Richard F. Bruguier was born Jan. 11, 1876 but died May 25 of the same year. In 1876 Francis added another drug store at 41 Bowery St. Their first daughter that we know of, Clara Hermine Bruguier, was born Feb. 26, 1879. Her birth certificate says she was the eighth child born to her parents, two surviving, so there are two other children we don't know about who must have died before then. They had a German live-in servant named Anna Beyla in the 1880 census at their house at 687 Market St. in Newark.

Sometime after 1872 Francis joined the Freemason organization Germania Lodge 128 F. and A.M. (Free and Accepted Masons). As a veteran of the Union Army, he joined the Lincoln Post 11 of the GAR (Grand Army of the Republic).

On July 26, 1881, Minnie Pauline Bruguier was born, and on Jan. 12, 1882, Clara died. Franz Alexander was born in April 1885 but died on July 15 of the same year. That year they lived at the corner of Lafayette and Hamburg St. The last child we have a record of was Francis A. Bruguier, Jr., born on June 11, 1888. My grandmother said that Oscar was educated in a private school. Knowing that the Bruguiers spoke German at home for another generation, I would expect this was a private German speaking school, and that Paul, Minnie and Frank also attended it. Newark had a large German immigrant population, and had such schools at that time.

In the 1900 census Francis and his family lived at 412 Lafayette St. in Newark, N.J. They had a live-in servant named Jennie Urick. Paul and Oscar had households of their own then. Minnie and Frank Jr. still lived at home. The 1900 census reported Francis and Anna had had 16 children. The census reported that only four survived to adulthood; Paul, Oscar, Minnie and Frank Jr. This was a time of high infant mortality rates but this rate is extremely high, and surprising considering Francis' profession of druggist and their comfortable financial situation. Perhaps my grandmother's account of her childhood illnesses can provide a possible cause: "My first recollection was waking up in an iron crib in a dining room, with the upper part of the windows pushed down so all the cold air could come in. All the doors to the bedrooms were closed, so the rest of the family could be warm. I had pneumonia and that was probably the treatment they used at the time." The house at 412 Lafayette St. is still standing; you can enter the address in Google Maps and see it using Google Street view.

In 1905 Francis was appointed to be a postal clerk in Newark. He was paid $400. Maybe people picked up their mail at the pharmacy. Francis and Anna were still living in their own household in the 1905 state census. My grandmother said that they lived on the third floor of her parents' house at 431 Lafayette St. (Oscar's family lived on the second floor; the first floor was for the pharmacy). He died at home (431 Lafayette St., Newark) of chronic intestinal nephritis on December 24, 1906 and was buried in the soldier's section of Fairmount Cemetery. Then his widow bought a double gravesite for them in 1908 in a different area of the cemetery. My grandmother remembered: "About the parlor, one scene I'll never forget – when my grandfather, Francis Bruguier died, his coffin was placed on the left wall next to the door where you entered the parlor and American flag was draped over his lower body with the words inscribed "Lincoln Post". I remember peeking over the top and seeing him so still but it never occurred to me to be frightened, it just was something that happened and I was just curious… He was a very tall man." She also told me that story when I was a child.

In Vol. 35 of the Proceedings of the Annual Meeting of the New Jersey Pharmaceutical Association, there was a one paragraph obituary of him. It said he had been ill four days, and that he "was an old and well-known pharmacist of Newark, having spent 38 years there….Joined the Association in 1878".   He also was listed in the Proceedings of the Masons of N.J. as a deceased member of Germania Lodge #128, 810 Broad St., Newark, which met the second and fourth Wednesdays.

In the 1910 census Anna lived with her son Frank, aged 21, and her son Oscar and his family. Her address was 431 Lafayette St., Newark City, 10th Ward. She moved in with her daughter Minnie on a farm in Hamburg, N.J. in 1913, and died there on December 8, 1915 of a ruptured appendix.

The obituary in the Newark Evening News says," BRUGUIER-Entered into rest on December 8, 1915, at Hamburg, N.J. Anna, widow of Francis Bruguier, aged 69 years. Relatives and friends are kindly invited to attend the funeral on Saturday, December 11, from the home of her son, Mr. Oscar Bruguier, 887 South Nineteenth Street, at 3 PM. Interment at Fairmount Cemetery."

Here are also a couple of photos of Francis and Anna after the 1860s, and photos of their monuments at Fairmount Cemetery in Newark, N.J.:

This one was sent to us by the German relatives, and was probably taken when Francis went back to visit his parents in the early 1870s.

THE FIFTH GENERATION

Our ancestor Oscar Richard Bruguier was the second surviving child of Francis and Anna. He was born on December 15, 1873 in Newark, N.J., barely a year after Paul. The story I heard from my grandmother was that he was studying to be a doctor at City College of New York, later renamed Columbia University, when he saw Mary Augusta Feldweg riding in the park, fell madly in love and dropped out of school to marry her. She was born in Newark on May 15, 1874 to Christian Robert Feldweg (known as Robert), a tinsmith who immigrated from Calw, Württemberg, and Amalie Bertha Auguste Mühlpfordt, (known as Bertha) born in Wittenberg, Saxony. Mary was a twin and her twin sister Julia died at age 3. Oscar and Mary were married on May 20, 1896 in Newark. The bride's parents signed as witnesses. This photo of Oscar and Mary was probably taken when they got married, or at about that time.

By the 1900 census they already had three little girls, Alma Bertha, born April 1, 1897, Lillian Mary, born August 30, 1898, and Irene Anna, born Jan. 4, 1900. They lived at 155 Hamburg Place in Newark, where he was a druggist. My grandmother Viola Elizabeth Bertha Bruguier was born next, on November 11, 1902. Her grandmother Bertha Feldweg had died exactly one year before, and perhaps that was a reason for Viola's middle name. The name Viola came from a local news story about a school girl by that name that was killed in a trolley accident. My grandmother did not like that name and my grandfather often called her Vi. Then came three boys: Harold Oscar, born July 12, 1905; Oscar Robert, called Bob, born September 23, 1908; and Warren Kenneth, born July 16, 1911. Warren was named after Oscar's friend, Dr. Warren. The baby of the family was Laverne Audrey, born February 23, 1918. All the children were born in Newark, N.J. Here is a photo of Oscar and Mary with the first five children. From left to right, the children are Viola , Lillian, Alma, Irene, and Harold. So this photo was taken around 1907.

There was another large photo my grandmother had that showed the four girls standing, with enormous white hair bows that stood up stiffly. Somehow that photo has become lost. Sometime between 1900 and 1906, the family moved to 431 Lafayette St. My grandmother recalled the apartment: "We lived over my father's pharmacy which stood on an apex, our street no. was 431 Lafayette St. It was a big apartment with a large kitchen and a coal range. The dining room was large and also the "parlor", which was only used on Sundays because it was furnished with beautiful furniture. I recall a chair painted gold which stood in a corner which was odd as it really was unusual, dainty and not too strong but really quite elegant. Then there was a sofa, upholstered, like a love seat and others I can't recall. The general appearance was so attractive, more for entertaining, probably the reason we saved it for Sundays where my Mother and Father read the Sunday papers and we read the funnies, like the "Katzenjammer Kids", etc." For breakfast they usually had a hard roll and a cup of half milk, half coffee.

On April 29, 1908, Oscar got a passport and spent three weeks going to Germany to visit relatives. He met his father's brother Otto near Berlin. Otto sent a fancy carriage with 6 or 8 horses and took him to his "castle on a hill" (as Oscar described it). Oscar returned from Bremen, Germany, arriving on July 28, 1908. Oscar was a druggist and his brother Frank worked in a toiletry factory, which must have been the Bruguier Chemical Company, which manufactured talcum powder, "Satin Skin peroxide cold cream", and "French antiseptic tooth powder" (see ads later). They had a "Bel Bon" line of toilet articles, and the trade name was discussed in a 1911 book called the Annual Convention of the Associated Advertising Clubs. The packaging was attractive and was illustrated in a 1913 book, The Graphic Arts, Vol. 5. The company was incorporated June 16, 1908. One would expect Oscar had returned or not yet left for Europe when it was incorporated. Advertisements were placed as far afield as Kansas City in 1914. The "factory" was a converted house at 76 Hamburg Place in Newark (renamed Wilson Ave. during WWI). It was a few houses away from their house. My grandmother remembered: "… when it was first established, the Henslers offered to "back" my father in his new venture "Bel Bon" and they hired a sales manager and first thing we knew they purchased a lavender or purple van which delivered orders. On the side of it was painted a big bouquet of violets and it was really attractive. At the exposition for manufacturers at the Newark Armory, the Bel Bon Co. had a booth and gave out as souvenirs, fans that resembled a bouquet of violets, with a handle to fan yourself in hot weather. Remember – they didn't have air conditioning those days. On the back of the fan it said:

"The thing that goes the farthest
With making life worthwhile
That costs the least and does the most
Is just a pleasant smile.
It's full of worth and goodness
If given with good intent
It's worth a million dollars
But doesn't cost one cent."
There, I had to go back in time when I learned this, 10-12 years old".

She continued: "But the sales manager was so freely spending Pa's money to promote the Bel-Bon Co… that he decided to take his formula that he concocted, so that was the end of the Bel-Bon Co. My French father had a temper and wouldn't let anyone to do as they wanted, without his consent. It was said he could have made a million with his formulas. Also made a "lotion of rosewater and glycerin – called Rose Cream Lotion" which were (sic) sold at a profit but not like Bel Bon."

Here are photos of a can of talcum powder they manufactured:

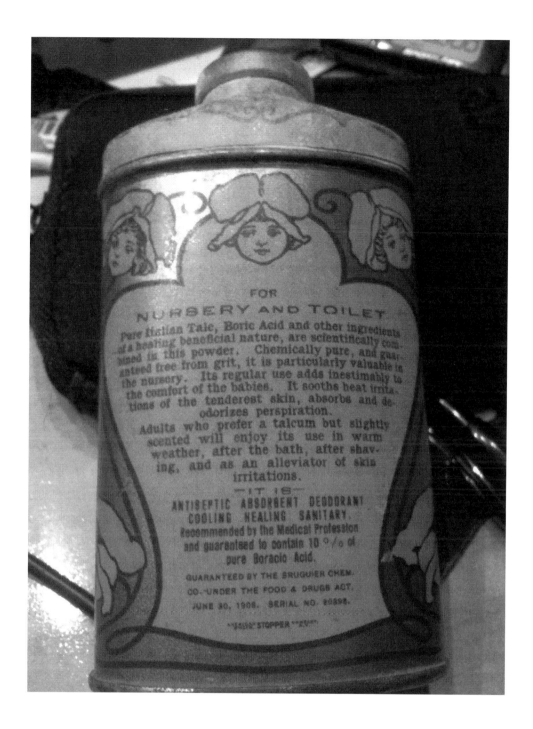

For

NURSERY AND TOILET

Pure Italian Talc, Boric Acid and other ingredients
of a healing beneficial nature, are scientifically com-
bined in this powder. Chemically pure, and guaranteed free from grit, it is particularly valuable in
the nursery. Its regular use adds inestimably to
the comfort of the babies. It sooths heat irritations of the tenderest skin, absorbs and de-
odorizes perspiration.

Adults who prefer a talcum but slightly
scented will enjoy its use in warm
weather, after the bath, after shav-
ing, and as an alleviator of skin
irritations.

—IT IS—

ANTISEPTIC ABSORBENT DEODORANT
COOLING HEALING SANITARY.

Recommended by the Medical Profession
and guaranteed to contain 10 °/o of
pure Boracic Acid.

GUARANTEED BY THE BRUGUIER CHEM.
CO.—UNDER THE FOOD & DRUGS ACT.
JUNE 30, 1906. SERIAL NO. 20898.

Despite being German and originally Lutheran, they attended the Sixth Presbyterian Church at 178 Lafayette St.

Oscar had to register for the draft two months before the end of WW1. He said he had his own drugstore at the corner of Lafayette and Wilson Ave. in Newark, was 5'6", slender, had grey eyes and grey hair, and lived at the house on 887 S. 19th St. that my mother knew. Sometime during WW1, someone threw a brick through the plate glass window of the Bruguier drug store. The family always attributed it to anti-German feeling. Newark did in fact have a large German immigrant population, especially of people from Württemberg. At that time there was so much anger at Germany that street names in Newark were actually changed from their former German names to English names. Notice above, for example, that Oscar's address on the draft card was Lafayette and Wilson, but it was actually the same building that formerly was Lafayette and Hamburg. It was after this that the Bruguiers started saying they were French, leading the younger generations to forget about their German roots. One strange thing they ate, that perhaps was German, was eels for dinner. They also ate sauerbraten, a vinegary pot roast dish, and almond crescent cookies at Christmas.

Here is the house at 887 S. 19th St., Newark, N. J. You can still see it on Google street view, where it looks far too small for ten people to live.

In 1920, Alma, Lillian and Irene lived at home but worked as stenographers or clerks. In 1930, they lived at the same address, with Bob, a bank clerk, Warren, a college student, and Laverne, 12. Oscar was 56 and still a druggist at a drug store. In 1940 they lived in the same house as in 1930, with their daughter Laverne, son Robert, his wife Margaret, and their son Ronald. Oscar, 66, was working as a druggist. Laverne was a clerk at an insurance company. Robert was a bookkeeper at an auto dealership. Oscar and Mary stayed in this house for the rest of their lives.

In the summers they would go to this house in Ocean Grove, N.J.:

Ocean Grove was a very strict Methodist town where cars were not allowed. One time Viola got in trouble for wearing her bathing suit, and was chased down the beach by the police! Presumably they did not catch her.

This photo was taken at Laverne's wedding on Sep. 6, 1941 to Ernie Hancox. Notice the bride is not front and center, as she would be today. In the front row are Irene(Field), Maida Trautweiler (groom's sister), Marguerite Snyder (groom's sister), Lillian (Steenburgh), Peggy Downs Bruguier, (Bob's wife), and Marie Hancox (groom's sister-in-law). In the back row are Alma (Rogers), Viola (Downs), Laverne (Hancox), Edna Bruguier (Warren's wife), Altha Bruguier (Harold's wife) and Gladys Hancox (groom's sister-in-law).

My mother told me Oscar used to pound his cane on the floor and say, "damn dose Nazis"!
She said that even though he and his wife lived their whole lives in New Jersey, they spoke
with German accents. She said on Sunday afternoons their children and grandchildren would
visit, and remembers big Christmas Eve parties with all the relatives in the basement of their
home.

Oscar died at his home at 887 South Nineteenth St. in Newark on Oct. 9, 1950 at 10:30 PM.
The death certificate says he had the medical condition which caused his death since Oct.
1949. No autopsy was performed. His wife Mary survived him for ten years. She crocheted
and made lace and doilies. She lived at the same home until her death on Nov. 28, 1960 and
was remembered as a loving grandmother. My mother said her grandmother would sneak her
and her sister each a nickel and say, "Don't tell Pa!"

Next is a photo of Mary on her 80th birthday, taken on May 15, 1954, with some of her children and grandchildren and their spouses.

From left to right:
Standing, rear row: Herbert Downs, Perce Rogers, Carl Parker, Joyce Downs Parker, Al Field Sr., Alma Rogers, Mary Feldweg Bruguier.
Seated, back row: Viola Bruguier Downs, Irene Bruguier Field, Jeanne Steenburgh Kvernland, Jack Kvernland, Lillian Bruguier Steenburgh.
Seated on floor: Iris Field, Al Field Jr., Peggy Downs Bruguiere, Ernie Hancox
Reclining: Bob Bruguiere.

This photo was taken in summer 1931, as it is Mary and Oscar with my mother Suzanne who was born in January 1931.

Our ancestor was my grandmother, Viola Elizabeth Bertha Bruguier, born Nov. 11, 1902 in Newark, N.J. She attended Madison Elementary School in Newark. Her parents had an eighth grade graduation party for her. Boys and girls brought chocolates, rolled up the rugs and danced. On her sixteenth birthday, World War I ended in 1918, and her birthday became Veteran's Day. She had blue, blue eyes and wavy brown hair. In high school she played the banjo, which surprised me since she once told me she didn't care much about music.

Two days after she graduated from East Side Commercial and Manual Training High School, she got a job working as a secretary at a law firm. After a few months her best friend asked her to apply for a position where she worked, the Jersey Central Railroad. The office was in Manhattan at Liberty and West St., later adjacent to the World Trade Center. One of the perks was free or reduced train tickets; she went to Montreal and another time to Vancouver, British Columbia with a girl friend. She earned $25 a week, which she gave to her father, and then he would give her back $10 and kept $15 for room and board. Viola worked there for five years. She also bobbed her hair, which made her father so upset, he wanted to throw her out of the house. Up until that time women always wore their hair long. At a dance she met my grandfather, Herbert Eugene Downs, born April 2, 1903 in Newark to Eugene Loomis Downs and Laura Eloise Ludlow Downs. He worked as a bank teller at the Fidelity Union Trust Company in Newark, where he had started sweeping the floors before he dropped out of Barringer High School to support his mother and sisters. Unlike the Bruguiers, the Downs family had been in America for three hundred years, but due to the separation or divorce of his parents in his childhood, Herb's family was not as well off as Viola's family. Viola was raised Lutheran and Herb was raised Baptist, but as a couple they belonged to the Presbyterian Church. This photo of Herbert was likely taken about the time they met.

After a courtship long enough for him to save enough to buy the furniture for their home, they were married on March 19, 1926 in Newark. My grandmother said, "I thought he'd never propose!" leading me to believe she married late but in fact she was only 23. My grandfather joked he had married an older woman since she was 5 months older. Here are a couple of photos of them from that time:

They started married life at 14 Peck Ave. in Newark but due to the Depression they moved in with her parents at 887 S. 19th St. My mother, Suzanne Bruguiere Downs was the first child born to them, on January 16, 1931 in Newark. She had green eyes and dark brown hair. Their second child was Joyce Diane Downs, born February 7, 1933 in Newark. Joyce had blue eyes and brown hair. Herbert had a good voice and was encouraged to audition to sing on the radio. However, it was during the Depression, and after waiting a while at the radio station, Herbert decided he'd better keep his secure bank job, and left before auditioning. He used to sing, "I had a dream, dear, you had one too..."

In 1935 they lived at 741 Midland Blvd., Townley, N.J., the first house they bought. Today Townley is part of Union, N.J. The house was built in 1929, 3 bedrooms, 1.5 baths, and sold recently for $250,000. You can see it on Google Maps Street view. They had to leave that house sometime after 1940 as they couldn't keep up the payments even though Herbert never lost his job at the bank.

About 1945 they moved to Chatham, N.J., a wealthier town, and lived at 25 Inwood Rd. Both daughters graduated from Chatham High School. After the girls married and moved away, Viola and Herb moved to Monmouth County, where they had relatives. They lived in Lincroft, N.J. but after a short while they moved to a brand new house at 40 Silverbrook Rd. in Shrewsbury, N.J., two doors down from Viola's brother Bob who was married to Herb's cousin Peggy. That was the house I spent vacations at, when we weren't at the beach, only 5 miles away.

Here is a photo from a reunion in 1965 at Bob and Peggy's house in Shrewsbury:
(L-R) Back row: Al Field, (Irene's husband), Bob Bruguier, Carl Parker (Joyce's husband), Jack Kvernland (Lillian 's son-in-law)
Front row: Alma, Irene, Gene Steenburgh (Lillian's husband), Herb Downs, Judy Hale Hancox (Laverne's daughter-in-law), Ernie Hancox (Laverne's husband), Susie Hancox (Laverne's daughter), Laverne, Peter Bruguiere (Bob's son), and Suzanne Downs (Viola 's daughter). Gene and Herb are fooling around in this photo.

Herb commuted by train to Fidelity Union Trust (bank) in Newark. He retired at age 65 and after my mother remarried they moved to Boynton Beach, Florida. Their hobbies were bridge, golf, embroidery, knitting, reading, swimming, and shuffleboard. They were very social people who had a lot of friends, visiting with someone almost every day. My grandmother visited the beach several times a week when they lived there. Herbert died of emphysema on his 79th birthday, April 2, 1982. After a year or two Viola moved to Lancaster, PA, where her daughter Joyce lived. She continued to be very active but Parkinson's disease slowed her down till she passed away on September 17, 2000, almost 98 years old.

THE SEVENTH GENERATION

Suzanne Bruguiere Downs, oldest child of Viola Bruguier and Herbert Fugene Downs, graduated from Chatham High School and attended Madison College in Virginia for two years, where she majored in Spanish. She loved to read and to write poetry, and loved jazz and opera. After college she moved back to Chatham and worked as a secretary in Manhattan at McGraw-Hill and U.S. Rubber. She married former high school classmate James Joseph Kirner on May 2, 1953 at Bainbridge Air Force Base in Georgia. They had known each other in high school but he was not one of her many beaux then. Jim was the son of Lee Kirner, an attorney in Chatham, and Agnes Vera Fennessy Kirner. Below you can see her high school portrait and a photo taken right after her wedding.

Here are their parents at the wedding:

The Korean War was on and Jim was a first lieutenant in the Air Force. Right after the wedding they were transferred to Lubbock, Texas, then Sacramento, California, and finally to Travis Air Force Base in California. Jim flew a hospital plane between Hawaii and California, bringing wounded soldiers back to the US for medical treatment. Suzanne and Jim had three children, Lise Joyce Kirner, and Marc James Kirner; Lise had a twin brother, James Kirner, Jr., who was still born. After the war, Jim studied law at UC San Francisco and became a lawyer. Suzanne and Jim divorced in 1964 after two separations.

Suzanne returned to New Jersey to be close to her parents in Monmouth County, and worked at Monmouth College and Progressive Life Insurance. Suzanne married a widowed coworker, Albert H. Kirms, on Aug. 13, 1967 in Bradley Beach, N.J. It was a second marriage for both of them. He had been active in county civic service and local offices since the 1940s and had responded to the Hindenburg explosion as a volunteer fire man. They separated in August 1970 and were divorced in 1972. Suzanne and the children returned to northern California, and she worked as a secretary, editor and journalist and lived in several states, settling near Show Low, AZ, then San Angelo, Texas, and finally Austin, Texas. She passed away from Parkinson's disease there on April 23, 2014.

Joyce Diane Downs attended college in New Hampshire. She married Carl Hahn Parker Jr. on April 17, 1955 in Chatham, N.J. Carl was from a Quaker family in Pennsylvania and attended college in Indiana. He was a salesman for Gibson Greeting Cards for most of his career. They had four children, Deborah Sue Parker, born in Red Bank, N.J., Cynthia Downs Parker, born in

Abington, PA, Carl Hahn Parker III (Chip) born in Abington, PA, and Todd Herbert Parker, born in Lancaster, PA. Joyce worked in a bank in Lancaster, PA for many years. She had a bubbly personality and loved to do arts and crafts and travel. She was active in her church, especially in the choir, which performed in Europe. After her mother Viola was too old to live alone, Joyce shared her home and cared for her. Joyce passed away from leukemia on Feb. 11, 2012. Below is a photo of Joyce (right) and I in front of her home in May 1993.

PART THREE: OTHER DESCENDANTS OF OSCAR RICHARD BRUGUIER

When young, Alma had thought of becoming a doctor, but her parents were not encouraging about a career in medicine. Alma married Percival (Perce) A. Steinmueller Rogers on June 23, 1920 and had two children, Blair Oakley Rogers, on Nov. 14, 1923, and Geraldine Bruguier,called Gerry, born Dec. 25, 1926. Perce had been a child vaudeville actor who shared the stage with Mae West. He worked at the US. Fidelity & Guarantee Co. for 49 years. Blair grew up to become a famous plastic surgeon. He used to send out long Christmas letters about his trips to Europe and encounters with the rich and famous. The above photo was taken about 1926.

Lillian married Eugene Masten Steenburgh, called Gene, on May 12, 1920 and had two children, Jeanne Audrey Steenburgh (Kvernland) on Aug 26, 1922, and Donald Rae Steenburgh, on Feb. 13, 1929. Eugene also worked in banking. This photo was taken on Sep. 6, 1941 at her sister Laverne's wedding.

Irene married a dentist, Dr. Albert Everett Field, on Oct. 8, 1924. They had two sons, who both became dentists, Albert E. Field, Jr., called Al, born March 18, 1927, and Richard Douglas Field, called Dick, born November 16, 1928. They lived on Long Island in New York. This photo was taken on Sep. 6, 1941. Irene was the aunt who sent birthday cards to a wide assortment of family members, even if they lived abroad. She lived to 100. Her husband, Uncle Bert, had a wonderful sense of humor.

Harold married Altha Bunnell Smith on Nov. 24, 1928. They had two sons and a daughter, Thomas Harold Bruguiere, born Apr. 8, 1930, Robert Smith Bruguiere, and Jane Bruguiere (Norton). This branch of the family used an "e" at the end of the name. Harold was a track coach at Plainfield (N.J.) High School and died relatively young, of cancer, on Oct. 19, 1954. Robert was a teacher who spent summer vacations working as a police officer on Martha's Vineyard. He was very much involved in the investigation of Sen. Edward Kennedy's Chappaquiddick accident that killed one of Kennedy's staffers. A Google search of "Patrolman Robert Bruguiere" will bring up many news stories and photos of him speaking to the press. Son Thomas moved to Virginia and managed an apple farm that had been in his wife's family for many decades.

Oscar Robert (Bob) met his wife at the wedding of his sister Viola. Viola's husband, Herbert Eugene Downs, had a cousin Peggy (Margaret Ruth) Downs. Oscar Robert went by Bob all his life. He married Peggy Downs on Oct. 5, 1930 in Butler, N.J. They had two sons, Ronald and Peter Robert. Bob and Peggy lived downstairs from his parents in the family home in Newark. He changed the spelling of his name to Bruguiere with an "e" on the end to avoid confusion with his father's name. Bob worked as a bookkeeper. Later Bob and Peggy moved to Silverbrook Rd. in Shrewsbury, N.J. Bob was a Civil War buff and had a boat, which we thought was terribly exciting. His son Ron worked in show business in New York and Hollywood as a manager, and published an autobiography titled "Collision". Peter was a school teacher. Here is a photo of Ron and Liza Minelli in 1961.

Warren married Edna Reuther on Nov. 29, 1935 and they had two daughters, Margot Mary , born Sep. 8, 1939 in Newark, and Christine. In 1964 they lived in Wellesley Hills, Massachusetts. He attended Columbia University, then worked for the S.C. Johnson Company as northeast sales manager. This photo was taken Apr. 9, 1933. He also changed the spelling of his name to Bruguiere. When my grandmother heard he had died, she wrote: "Had such a sad "gone" feeling when I heard the news. Perhaps it's better we remember him as he was. Strong-looking – affable and always glad to see us."

Laverne Audrey, the youngest of Oscar and Mary's children, married Ernest (Ernie) Hancox on Sep. 6, 1941. They had two children, Robert Ernest Hancox and Susan Lynne Hancox. This photo was taken on her wedding day.

PART FOUR: OTHER DESCENDANTS OF FRANCIS AND ANNA BRUGUIER

PAUL CHARLES BRUGUIER AND HIS DESCENDANTS

Francis and Anna's oldest surviving child was Paul Charles Bruguier, born October 11, 1872 in Newark, N.J. He worked as a machine pattern maker most of his life. He married Mary Boehm on March 31, 1896 and they had ten children. In 1900 they lived at 431 Lafayette Street in Newark (with his parents). At that time they had two daughters, Edna Mae and Wilhelmina Minerva (Minnie), born August 20, 1896 and May 23, 1899, respectively. In 1910 he was a wood pattern maker at a factory in Newark. The family had additional children, Arthur A., born July 26, 1901, Paul O., born Sep. 22, 1903, Eleanor Maybell, born May 9, 1907, and Charles Roy, born Dec. 19, 1908. Later they had Lorraine D. , born Dec. 15, 1911, and Wilbur, born in 1917, who died in the 1920s. Just before the end of WWI Paul had to register for the draft, and said he was a pattern maker at Haws and Phillips in Newark, but lived in Hawthorne, N.J. He was of medium height and build, with grey eyes and light colored hair. In 1920 he lived in Hawthorne at 38 Fourth Ave, still working as a pattern maker; Arthur and Paul worked for the rail road. In 1930 they lived in Raritan, part of West Keansburg, in Monmouth County, N.J. At that time he worked as a carpenter in the thread industry. On 20 May 1934, he died in Dover, N.J. and is buried in Fair View Cemetery in Middletown, N.J. The family story is that he was mowing his son's lawn when he died of a heart attack. His wife died on July 28, 1942 and is buried with him. (His brother Frank is also buried in that cemetery).

Paul's daughter Edna married Victor Lish and had two children, Edna Mae Lish, born May 12, 1916, and Victor Robert Lish, born Aug. 12, 1917. Victor worked as accounting manager at a life insurance company in Nutley, N.J. in 1940. He was the grandfather of genealogist Mary Lish.

Daughter Wilhelmina Minerva, known as Minnie, married Patrick Halloran and had six children, Eleanor, born about 1919; Katherine M.. and Winifred M., twins, born Apr. 22, 1920 in Columbiana, Ohio; Michael J., born Aug. 9, 1922 in Columbiana, Ohio; Lorraine Eileen, born Apr. 10, 1928 in Long Branch, N.J.; and Patrick J., born about 1930. In 1940, Patrick worked as a laborer in the Middletown, N.J. sanitation department.

Son Arthur A. was born July 26, 1901 and married Dorothy Koemmel. His wife died quite young, leaving only one child, George Arthur, born Dec. 29, 1929. Arthur was an auto mechanic in 1940 in Keansburg, N.J. His son George was a genealogist who collaborated with several of us to help fill in the story of Paul's side of the family. His son Michael now has Francis Bruguier's sword and a 25th anniversary plate once belonging to Francis and Anna.

Son Paul O. was born Sep. 22, 1903 and married Elsa A. Shumacher. His 50th wedding anniversary was featured in the Red Bank Daily Register July 17, 1975 with a photo of the couple who lived in West Keansburg, N.J. He did not have any children. Paul worked as a sign hanger in 1940.

Son Warren F. was born in January 1906 but only lived a couple of months. This was sad but not unusual at that time.

Daughter Eleanor Maybell was born May 9, 1907. She married Albert M. Jennings and had a daughter, Jeanne Edna, born Jan. 16, 1931. They lived in Middletown, N.J. and Albert worked as a clerk at Prudential Insurance in 1940.

Son Charles Roy was born Dec. 19, 1908. He married Leonore A. Burke and had two children, Yvonne S., born about 1936, and Leroy Bruguier, born about 1946. On May 14, 1942, he was injured at his job as a still operator at Merck in Rahway and sued the company for injuries to his digestive system caused by inhaling fumes. The incident necessitated an operation and Charles' lawyer obtained an out of court settlement of $1,500, which is equivalent to about $22,500 today. The case went to the New Jersey state supreme court. After 1946, Charles and Leonore divorced, and then Charles married Maurice Dee Lennon, nee Mooney. They had son Richard Charles and daughters Mary and Elsa. Charles' divorce case is referenced in law books as Bruguier v. Bruguier and relates to a child's ability to assume the name of a step parent.

Daughter Lorraine was born Dec. 15, 1911. She married William Rauch and had a son, William Rauch III. William worked at a bank in Keansburg, N.J. in 1930.

Son Wilbur was born about 1917 and died about 1920.

MINNIE BRUGUIER AND HER DESCENDANTS

Francis and Anna's only surviving daughter, Minnie, married three times and was widowed three times. Minnie Pauline Bruguier was born in Newark, N.J. on July 26, 1881. In 1900 she worked as a sales lady in a dry goods store. Her first husband, Marcus S. Henderson, was a 32 year old widower with at least two children. He was born on July 3, 1868 in New Jersey. He was a farmer who lived in Hardyston, Sussex County, New Jersey, about 40 miles northwest of Newark. They married on August 26, 1900 in Newfoundland, Morris County, N.J. They had 6 children, Clara A., born July 22, 1902, Francis Bruguier, born Feb. 23, 1905, Beatrice E., born May 28, 1908, Iona Wilhelmina born Jan. 1, 1913, Kenneth Marcus, born April 7, 1915, and Marie Audrey, born July 5, 1921. My grandmother remembers going to stay with them in the summers. She said there were so many children that they slept head to foot, several in a bed. Unfortunately Marcus died of heart failure on July 8, 1924 at the age of 56. He was buried at North Hardyston Cemetery in Hamburg, Sussex Co., N.J., as was she and her next two husbands.

Minnie remarried, to widower John Denike, seven years her senior, in the 1920s. In the 1930 census she and the three youngest children lived with him at 287 Vernon Ave. in Hamburg, Sussex County, where he worked as a landscape laborer. He died on January 29, 1933.

By 1935 Minnie married a third time, to James Day, a school janitor nine years older than she. In 1940 they lived on Clark St. in Ogdensburg, Sussex County, N.J., where they had lived since at least 1935. He died February 5, 1952 in Trenton, N.J. Minnie died at in March 1977 at age 95, in Frankford, N.J. and was survived by all six of her children.

Minnie and Marcus' daughter Clara married Roy Benjamin Casterlin, a fireman. They had no children. They lived in Sussex Co., N.J.

Son Francis Bruguier married Helen Shauger and had five children, Helen, born about 1930; Kenneth M., born Oct. 9, 1932; Willina/Wilhelmina P., born about 1937; Roy B., born about 1939, and Francis, born in 1943. In 1940 he was a laborer in the Dutch Elm project, living in Wantage, N.J.

Daughter Beatrice E. was born May 28, 1908. She married Floyd C. Day and had three children, Helen M., born about 1927, Virginia V., born about 1929, and Allen, born about 1931. They moved to the Hartford, Connecticut area about 1936. In 1940 he was a machine operator at Pratt & Cady Co., in Hartford, Connecticut. Unlike most married women at that time, who kept house, Beatrice worked as a waitress.

Daughter Iona W. was born Jan. 1, 1913. She married Albert Havens Casterlin, a roofer, and had four children, Mahlon Roy, born July 18, 1931; Delores, born about 1934; Reginald Dean, born about 1937; and Clara, born about 1939. Unfortunately Albert died in 1947 and Iona married a Mr. Martin some time later.

Son Kenneth Marcus . was born about 1915. He married Margaret and had two sons, Kenneth M. Jr., born about 1936, and Edward W., born about 1939. In 1940 he lived next door to his brother Frank and was also a laborer in the Dutch Elm project.

Daughter Marie Audrey was born July 5, 1921. She married a Mr. Toth.

FRANCIS BRUGUIER JR. AND HIS DESCENDANTS

The youngest of the four surviving children of Francis and Anna Bruguier was Francis A. Bruguier, Jr. (Frank). He was born in Newark, N.J. on June 11, 1888. About 1910 he married Mary Berry, nicknamed Mae. When he registered for the draft in WWI, he was a farm hand in Oak Tree, N.J. He was described as being tall, slender, with blue eyes and brown hair. Frank and Mae had children Dorothy Mae, born in 1911, Helen T. , born in 1912, and Edmund Francis, born February 25, 1915. In the 1920 census he lived at 103 Fairmount Ave. in Newark, where he was chauffeur at an auto company. By 1930 they had moved to Fourth Ave. in Keansburg, N.J., where Frank's oldest brother Paul lived. Frank worked as a mechanic at an auto shop. They lived next door to Edward Berry, Mae's father. In 1942 when Frank registered for the draft, he lived at 58 Ramsey Ave. in Keansburg and worked for the Titeflex Metal Hose Company in Newark. The commute can be explained by the fact that he was unemployed at least half the year in 1940. He was 5 foot 8 and a half inches tall, and 156 and a half pounds at that time.

Mae died on July 20, 1957 in Keansburg, and Frank lived there until 1961. He died in Neptune on July 9, 1962.

Daughter Dorothy married Rudolph Fred (Rudy) Heinzinger on June 8, 1930 in Keansburg. They had six children, Dorothy Mae (Dolly), born about 1934; Rudy Jr., born about 1938; twins Richard Charles and Ronald Frank; Robert; and a daughter. Rudy was foreman at a Monmouth County bakery in 1940, later becoming a driver for the Continental Baking Co., then salesman for Wonder Bread in Daytona Beach, Florida.

Daughter Helen married Joseph H. Calver, Jr. and had sons Joseph Henry, born Aug. 13, 1933 and Gary Richard, born May 24, 1938. In 1940 they lived in Red Bank, N.J. and he was a truck driver for a moving company. She was widowed in 1961.

Son Edmund Francis was born Feb. 25, 1915. In 1940 he was single, living in Neptune, N.J., and working as a salesman for a bakery. He married Helen Joanna Gamble and had a daughter Sandra. He moved to Florida some time before 1960.

PART FIVE: OTHER DESCENDANTS OF CARL FRIEDRICH ALEXANDER VON BRUGUIER

Of Alexander and Hermine's six children, three did not live to adulthood. The youngest son, Friedrich Wilhelm Julius Otto von Bruguier, married but had no children.

EMMA VON BRUGUIER AND HER DESCENDANTS

Emma was two years younger than our immigrant ancestor Franz/Francis von Bruguier. She married Wilhelm Arlt on November 5, 1867 in Baerwalde in Neumark. Although today called Mieszkowice in Poland, at the time it was part of Prussia. Their children were Meta Luisa Hermine Elisabeth, born Aug. 25, 1868; Emma Berta Margarete, born Jan. 7, 1870; Hans, born July 10, 1871; Walda, born June 13, 1875; Wilhelm, born June 25, 1877 in Stettin, Pomerania, today's Szczecin, Poland, a large city near the Baltic Sea and today's German/Polish border; Erich, born Oct. 4, 1878; Willy, born July 1, 1880; Meta Hulda Gertrud, born Apr. 15, 1883; and Max Otto Erwin, born Sep. 14, 1885. Emma, Walda, Wilhelm and Erich did not survive early childhood.

When Oscar Bruguier went to Germany, he met Otto von Bruguier and Erwin Arlt, who corresponded with Oscar's daughter Alma Bruguier Rogers in the early 1960s regarding the German and French origins of the family. Erwin sent us the photos of Alexander, Hermine, Franz and Anna, and transcriptions of their family Bible records.

PART SIX: ASSOCIATED FAMILIES IN MY DIRECT LINE

Francis Bruguier's wife Anna Ladewig was the daughter of Edward Ladewig and Wilhelmina (nicknamed Minna) Rabach of Brandenburg, the kingdom centered in today's Berlin, Germany. Edward was born on Apr. 10, 1811. Minna was born Feb. 2, 1814 in Brandenburg. Edward came to New York before his wife and children. He first worked as a light house keeper in Brooklyn. Wilhelmina and children Gustav A., born Feb. 5, 1839, Maria Louise, born Jan. 5, 1843, and Anna Wilhelmina, born Aug. 23, 1846, arrived in New York City on board the Herschel on Jul. 27, 1855. There were only a few Ladewigs in New York City at that time but it was not an uncommon name in Brandenburg. By 1865 they had moved to Castleton, Staten Island, N.Y., where Edward worked in various positions relating to light houses. Edward died on July 12, 1898, leaving several houses on Staten Island to his daughters and the children of his son Gustav, who had died in 1870. Maria married Gustav Mueller and had five children. Edward and Minna are buried at Woodland Cemetery in Castleton, Staten Island, N.Y.

Oscar Bruguier's wife Marie Augusta Feldweg was the daughter of Christian Robert Feldweg (Robert) and Amalie Bertha Auguste Mühlpfordt. Robert was born on Feb. 8, 1849, in Calw, Württemberg, a small mountain town near the border of southern France. At that time Württemberg was a separate country. Robert immigrated to Newark, N.J. soon after his mother's death and father's remarriage, in July 1869. There he met Bertha, who was born in Wittenberg, Sachsen-Anhalt, also a separate country, on Aug. 1, 1840. Her father, Johannes Carl A. Mühlpfordt (Charles Milford), a tailor, had come to Newark and remarried in 1857. Bertha and her brother Oskar followed separately. Bertha arrived here on May 7, 1868 and married Robert on Nov. 7, 1869. My grandmother told me Bertha's father told her if she married, he would never talk to her again. She said he just wanted her to take care of his children by his new wife. It's possible he also thought she was marrying hastily; however, at that time, an unmarried woman of 29 was considered an old maid and was of low social status. Robert was a tinsmith and he and Bertha had Elizabeth, born in Aug. 1870; twins Marie and Julia, born May 15, 1874; Robert Jr., born Oct. 13, 1876; and Bertha, born Feb. 28, 1879. Robert and Bertha are buried in Woodland Cemetery in Newark, N.J.

Viola Bruguier's husband Herbert Eugene Downs was the son of Eugene Loomis Downs and Laura Eloise Ludlow. Eugene was born on May 20, 1869 in Cedar Co., Iowa. The Downs family was actually from New Haven, Connecticut but they had moved for a few years to Iowa. Laura was born Nov. 18, 1871 in Rahway, N.J. Eugene and Laura had children Mabel Edna, born May 30, 1892; Ethel May, born June 16, 1894; Dorothy Eloise, born Dec. 15, 1897; and Herbert Eugene, born Apr. 2, 1903, all in Newark, N.J. Eugene worked as a salesman in various industries and also owned a Nash automobile dealership for a while. He was an agent for Trumbull cars in 1915 and sold the Owen Magnetic Car in 1918, before he sued that company and won at the state Supreme Court level. Eugene and Laura separated when Herbert was about seven years old, and Herbert dropped out of high school to support his mother and sisters by working at the Fidelity Union Trust, where he spent his entire working life, ending as Treasurer. Viola and Herbert are buried at the First Presbyterian Churchyard in Shrewsbury, N.J., the church they attended.

Suzanne Bruguier Downs' first husband was James Joseph Kirner, son of Leo Jeremiah (aka Lee Francis) Kirnerand Agnes Vera Fennessy. James was born on Mar. 15, 1931 in Summit, N.J. Leo Jeremiah Kirner was born in Jersey City, N.J. on Dec. 13, 1896 and went by Lee Francis Kirner as an adult. He had a cotton brokerage in New York City, was active in N.J. local politics in the 1930s, and became a lawyer in the 1940s. Although he had a German name, his family was almost entirely Irish. Agnes Vera Fennessy was born in Jersey City, N.J. Aug. 5, 1898, daughter of a policeman. Lee and Agnes were parents of only two living children, Mary Lee Kirner born Feb. 23, 1921, and James Joseph. Lee is buried at Holy Name Cemetery in Jersey City, N.J.; Agnes is buried at George Washington Memorial Park in Paramus, N.J.

APPENDICES

List of Bruguier births and deaths from Bruguier family Bible(s):

The list appears to be on stationery from 1894. Notice the little crosses. That is a symbol used in German documents to show deaths. This was said to have been sent to us by cousin Gerda in Germany, but perhaps she got it from Oscar's family, since the headings are in English. It shows that the relatives continued their relationship despite living on different continents.

Oktober 1960 (ca.)

Dear Mrs Rogers!

It was just on my 75th birthday, that quite unexpected I got your letter dated 10th of September. I was very pleased to get a token sign of life of our relations in U.S.A after so long years. I remember very well the visit of your father Oskar, I think it was in 1927 or 1928, I was not yet married at that time; my eldest sister Elisabeth Brühl (whose husband died after the first world-war) lived with her daughter in my house. And since that visit of your father the connexion to our relations on the other side of the ocean was torn. Only my youngest sister Gertrud had changed letters with your aunt Milly, who sent her her photo (lost during the war).

Now you ask some details of the family of Bruguier.

I regret, that we don't know much of our ancestors of my mother's side. But my sister has some notes which I write down as follows: ✳ ———————————→

These are the few declarations I can give you.

In the mean time I have written to an authority that knows something about French families who emigrated to Germany (probably emigrated our family about the year 1685). Perhaps this authority are able to give us some more news concerning our ancestors. If this case happens, I shall give you some more news.

With many greetings to you and your family I am

yours sincerely Erwin Arlt

1) Francis August was born at Senftenberg in Niederlausitz, where his brothers and sisters were also born.

2) The names of the children were as follows:

  a) Francis born 23rd May 1841, baptized 4. of July 1841.

  b) Berta, Luise, Agnes, Emma (my mother) born 14. of May 1843, baptized 18. of June 1843, died 18. of September 1919.

  c) Rudolphe born 14. of May 1844, died Oktober 1944.

  d) Paul born 22. of September 1845 died 1945

  e) Friedrich Wilhelm, Julius, Otto, born 23. of July 1857
                                          baptized 16. of August 1857
                                          died 1945?

3). He was married with Anna Katharina Brehm 1895, who died 16. of April 1929. Otto had no children Emma (my mother) had 10 children. She was married 5. of November 1867 at Bärwalde i/ Neumark. To Wilhelm (William) Arlt born 30. August 1937 at Goschütz near Festenberg in Silesia. The 10 children were as follows:

  a) Meta, Luise, Hermine, Elisabeth, born 25. of August 1868, baptized 22. Sept. 1868, died during 2. war.

  b) Emma, Berta, Margarete, born 7. of January 1870, baptized 27. of February, died 1. of January

  c) Hans Arlt, born 10. of July 1871, baptized 6. of August 1871, died 29. of December 1941.

  d) Emma, born 18. of Dezember 1872, died 11. of Dezember 1874.

  e) Walda born 13. of June 1875, died 1877. 18 of June 1877.

f) Georg, born 25. of June 1877, died 8. of February 1878.

g) Erich born 4. of Oktober 1878, died 29. of May 1879

h) Willy born 1. of July 1880, died 19. of June 1926

i) Meta, Hulda, Gertrud (my sister still living in my house)
   born 15. of April 1883, baptized 12. of August 1883

k) Max, Otto, Erwin (myself) born 14. of September 1885.

4) The father of your grandfather Francis Bruguier was
Alexander von Bruguier. He was married to Hermine Kleinholz,
born 28. of July 1819 at Alt-Döbern i/Mark Brandenburg.
Alexander was born 29. of Oktober 1814 at Jülich a/ Rhein
His father was Karl Joseph von Brugie Bruguier, born
29. of April 1786, Captain at Jülich in Prüssia and later on
at Potsdam, died 28. Dezember 1845, was married to Henriette
Negendank, born 19. of January 1790 in Berlin, died
10. of Dezember 1844 at Charlottenburg (near Berlin)

Father of Karl Joseph von Bruguier was Johann von
Bruguier, Captain in service of Empire und Kingdom
Austria, died 20. of August 1794 in Regiment von Stain
near Mailant (Milano in Italy) in war

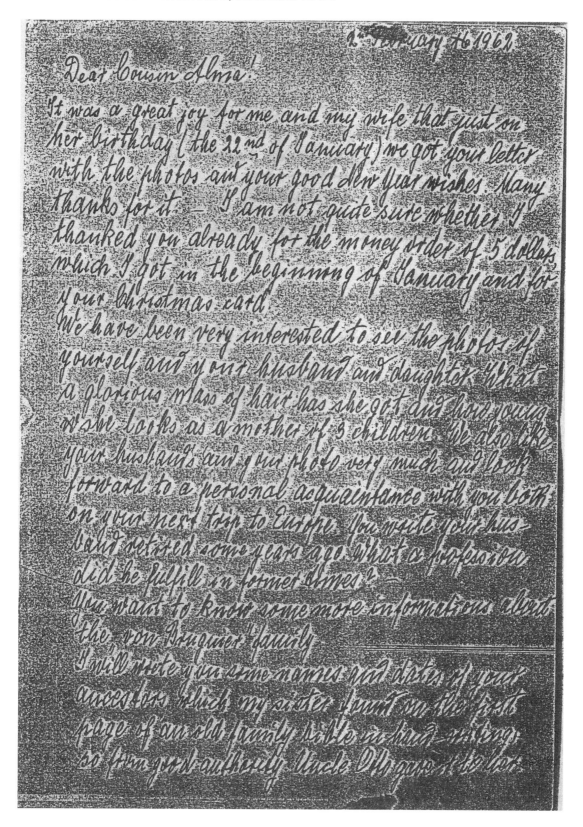

2nd February 1962

Dear Cousin Alma!

It was a great joy for me and my wife that just on her birthday (the 22nd of January) we got your letter with the photos and your good New Year wishes. Many thanks for it. – I am not quite sure whether I thanked you already for the money order of 5 dollars which I got in the beginning of January and for your Christmas card.

We have been very interested to see the photos of yourself and your husband and daughter. What a glorious mass of hair has she got! And how young she looks as a mother of 3 children. We also like your husband's and your photo very much and look forward to a personal acquaintance with you both on your next trip to Europe. You write your husband retired some years ago. What a profession did he fulfill in former times?

You want to know some more informations about the von Bauquier family.

I will write you some names and dates of your ancestors which my sister found on the first page of an old family bible in hand writing so from good authority. Uncle [...] gave it to her.

Our mother always told us, that she proceeded
from a French family of Hugenottes.
My mother Emma's great grand father was:

Johann von Bouguier, captain in Austrian
army, died in war 20th of August 1794 near
Milan

The grand father of my mother was named

Karl Joseph von Bouguier born 29th of April
1786

He was captain in the Prussian army at Jülich,
later he was sent to Potsdam where he died
the 28th of December 1845. He was married to
Henriette born Negendank in Berlin. They had
2 children: Alexander and Bertha von Bouguier.

The father of my mother was the just named

Alexander von Bouguier born 29th of October 1844
at Jülich on the Rhine. My mothers aunt Bertha
was born 1828 in August.

Why the father of my mother did not keep the
tradition of his forefathers to become an officer
                    ancestors
we do not know. Probably he had at first a
property in the country near Bremen and at
Hamburg, later on he lived as an official.

(Kanzleirat in German) at Landsberg on Warthe near Küstrin (Neumark, a fortress in former times) He married Hermine Kleinholn born the 28 th of July 1819. They lived at first at Senftenberg in Nieder Lausitz where the children were born:

1. Franz   born 23 d of May 1841 (when did he die ?)

2. Berta, Luise, Agnes, Emma (my mother) born 14 th of May 1843 died 18 th of October 1919

3. Rudolph born 14 th of May 1844 died October 1844

4. Paul   born 22 nd of September 1845 died 1845

5. Richard born 27 th of October, died 1856

6. Friedrich Wilhelm, Julius Otto born 23 d of July 1857 died 1946 married 1895 with Anna Catharina Brehm, who died 1929

My Uncle Otto was a geometrician, as my father also was. The title „von" Bruguier must have been in the family since long days. We thought that Uncle Frank renounced in America on this title on account of reasons we did not know.

Meanwhile you got perhaps a letter from my niece Gerda Brühl, daughter of my oltest sister (+ 1945). She wanted to write her your address because she thought you might be able to help her in an embarrassment of difficulty.. She is the single member of our family who changed her religion to the Roman Catholic Church.

This letter wrote my sister because she knows English better than I do.

With best wishes for you and your husband
your cousin

Erwin Abel

1.)

October, 5th, 1962

Dear Alma!

I think you are still waiting for this letter.
But it was impossible for me to write earlier.
When I came home finally — three weeks ago —
I had to arrange so many things with my clothes;
and I made eight parcels, most of them to East-
Germany. And I had to do all this immediately
because I am to go once more to the old lady
in Tutzing, where I was working last winter.
She has found no good nurse meanwhile and so she
begged me hardly to come again. Before I leave
my home to-morrow, you will be answered now.

I send you 4 fotos. They belong to my
cousin Magda in Osnabrück. She sends you kind
regards! She would like to get the fotos back,
and so you can send them to me, after having got
some foto-copies of these pictures, if you like them.
On the backside of the fotos you can find where
they have been made; — that of your dear mother
in New York / N.Y. / that of your father still in Berlin;
that of your grandfather in Landsberg / Warta.
Their names are written in an old script on the front;
Your grandparents: Alexander Friedrich Karl of B.
(= A. Frederick Charles) and Mrs. Henriette of B.

her whole name: Henriette, Sophie, Hermine of B.,
born Kleinholz.

I am sorry that I could not find another
foto which I remember from my childhood to
have seen it at my grandmother's. It represented
your parents with all their children! The girls had
big, stiff hair-ribbons and "corkscrew-curls",
but of course I did not know at that time
which of them was you! — This picture must have
been lost, it was so nice and much bigger
than these four which I send you.

Now I will try to answer your questions.
The profession of "Uncle Otto" — your father's
brother — was that of a surveyor in a higher
grade, an official of the State. (In German
we call him "Regierungsrat".)

Nobody knows why in old ages the
kings have given the title of nobility to
some persons, which is known by the small
word "de" (= of.) These men may have distin-
guished themselves during the war by bravery
or in the sciences by cleverness. This nobility
was the more important the older it was.
The family itself would like themselves very
much to know this reason!

3)

It is the same thing with the name of the French town from which your ancestors emigrated. I am sorry; nobody knows it.

But concerning the time of the emigration Magda has another theory than Aunt Gertrud. Gertrud thinks that the Bruguiers emigrated about 1685 after the annulment of the "Edict of Nantes" (which law had granted liberties for the Evangelic population in France.) In this case your ancestors would have been Protestants who emigrated because of their religious confession.

Magda supposes, however, that the emigration of the Bruguiers took place in the time of the Grand French Revolution of 1789! This theory has much more probability for itself, because the first "de Bruguier" whom we know, Johannes (= John) de Bruguier was Catholic. He may have emigrated because of the general hatred of the French people against the nobility in that bad times (you know: The guillotine!) And because he was Catholic he went with we suppose his family to a Catholic country which was Austria. He died as a captain in Austrian services 1794 in the fortress of Mailand /Italy; I suppose during the war.

4) His son already must have converted to the Protestants. It is Josef Karl de Bruguier who is called _Lutheran_ in the old notes and who became an officer in Prussian services; you know that Prussia is a country of Evangelic confession – and in the old times the two confessions were severely separated! This man is your great-grandfather (and mine, too.)

So dear cousin, this is all I can tell you, and I hope that some of these remarks may be useful to the genealogist working for your son.

In Bremen I was proud to show the two nice pictures you gave me. (I looked once more at Arlt's foto from you and saw that the pretended short only were an apron!)

I do hope that you both had a good time at the seaside and that your pains in the back have ceased or relaxed? Do you still wear your girdle? A friend of mine has lost these same pains by a girdle and a good diet! The doctor had told her to drink much milk, to eat little or no salt (this you will know yourself!) and to eat no pork and no fructified eggs (one must buy them from a woman who has no cock.)

I send some stamps for your husband and many, many greetings for both of you.

Yours sincerely

cousin Gerda

good health for you!

This is to certify that

Mr. *C.E. Francis A Brugaier* a *single man* *24* years of age,
a *merchant,* and native of *the Kingd: Prussia,* and
Miss *Ann Wilh.ma Ladewig,* a *single woman 19* years of age,
and a native of *Brandenburg (Kingd: Prussia)* both residing
now in the ~~City of~~ *State of Jersey* were *lawfully*
joined together into the holy matrimony on this *27* day of *February*
in the year of our Lord One thousand eight hundred and sixty *Six.*

The parties were identified by witnesses:

Mr. *Gustavus Ladewig*
Miss *Mary Ladewig*

In testimony whereof I, the officiating minister have set hereunto
my hand and seal.

Place where marr. *Pastor's residence*

N. Charles Schramm,

Pastor of the Protestant Episcopal Congregation of
St. George's German Chapel.

Residence: 91 2d St., N. Y.

FRANCIS' DEATH CERTIFICATE:

State of New Jersey—Bureau of Vital Statistics.
CERTIFICATE AND RECORD OF DEATH.

ANNA LADEWIG BRUGUIER'S DEATH CERTIFICATE:

OSCAR AND MARY'S MARRIAGE CERTIFICATE FROM ST. JOHN'S SECOND GERMAN LUTHERAN CHURCH, PASTOR WM. RIEB:

MINNIE'S BIRTH CERTIFICATE:

DEC. '80.

STATE OF NEW JERSEY.

BIRTH RETURN.

SEE PENALTY FOR NON-REPORT.

1. Full name of Child (if any).. Color *White*
2. Date of Birth............*July 26th 1881* Sex *Female*
3. Place of Birth............*Market St*
   (If city, give name, street and number; if not, give township and county.)
4. Name of Father............*Francis Bruguier* {If out of wedlock, write O. W.}
5. Maiden name of Mother............*Anna Ludwig*
6. Country of Father's Birth............*Germany* Age *40* Occupation *Druggist*
7. Country of Mother's Birth............*Germany* Age *34*
8. Number of Children in all by this Marriage............*9* How many Living *4*
9. Name and P. O. address of Medical Attendant in his own handwriting, with date,

BRUGUIER, Minnie P.   26 July, 1881   *Francis Bruguier + Anna Ludwig*

Notice "number of children in all by this marriage, 9, how many living, 4", 15 years after the marriage.

PAUL'S MARRIAGE CERTIFICATE:

STATE ~~OF NEW JERSEY~~

RETURN OF MARRIAGE

SEE PENALTY FOR NON-REPORT WITHIN 30 DAYS.

☞ Use Ink and write plainly, especially names.

1. FULL NAME OF HUSBAND.......
   (If colored, so state.)

2. Place of Residence.......
   (If in city, give name, street and number,
   if not, give township and county.)

3. Age....years....months. Number of his Marriage....

4. Occupation.......

5. Country of Birth.......

6. Name of Father.......
   Country of Birth.......

7. Maiden Name of Mother.......
   .... Country of Birth.......

8. FULL MAIDEN NAME OF WIFE.......
   (If colored, so state.)

9. Country of Birth.......

10. Place of Residence.......
    (If in city, give name, street and number,
    if not, give township and county.)

11. Age, nearest birthday.......

12. If in any trade or business so state.......

13. Last name, if a widow.......

14. Number of Bride's Marriage....

15. Name of Father.......
    Country of Birth.......

16. Maiden Name of Mother.......
    .... Country of Birth.......

17. Date (in full).......189..

18. Place of Marriage.......
    (City or township and county.)

19. In presence of { _(Be sure to have witnesses.)_

20. Signature of Minister
    (who Church Pastor of)
    or person officiating.

NOTE—All the facts called for in this Blank are important and
should be accurately given.

MINNIE'S FIRST MARRIAGE CERTIFICATE:

STATE OF NEW JERSEY.

H26

MARRIAGE RETURN.

SEE PENALTY FOR NON-REPORT WITHIN 30 DAYS.

Use Ink and write plainly, especially names.

1. FULL NAME OF HUSBAND. *Marcus S. Henderson*

Place of Residence. *Stockholm* *New Jersey.* (If Col., so state.)

2. Age *32* years *1* months. Number of his Marriage *2nd*

3. Occupation *Farmer* Country of Birth *America*

4. Name of Father *Matthias Henderson* Country of Birth ....

5. Maiden Name of Mother *Sarah Dunn* Country of Birth ....

II. MAIDEN NAME OF WIFE

Minnie P. Burgesser Country of Birth .... (If Col., so state.)

2. Place of Residence. *Newark N.J.* (If in city, give name, street and number; if not, give township and county.)

3. Age, nearest birthday. *19* (If in any trade or business, so state.)

4. Last name, if a Widow .... Number of Bride's Marriage *1st*

5. Name of Father *Francis Burgiss* Country of Birth *America*

6. Maiden Name of Mother *Anna Ladwig* Country of Birth ....

1. Date in full *August 26th 1900* Place *New foundland N.J.* (City or township and county.)

2. In presence of *Lama Fountain / Edna F. Slater* (Be sure to have witnesses)

3. Signature of Minister, what Church Pastor of or person officiating. *Geo Fountain Pastor New foundland M.E. Church*

All the facts called for in this Blank are important, and should be accurately given.

OSCAR'S DEATH CERTIFICATE:

MARY'S DEATH CERTIFICATE:

STATE DEPARTMENT OF HEALTH OF NEW JERSEY   48979

1. PLACE OF DEATH	2. USUAL RESIDENCE (Where deceased lived. If institution; residence before admission).
a. COUNTY Essex	a. STATE New Jersey b. COUNTY Essex

b. CITY ☐ BOROUGH ☐ (Check box and give name) TOWNSHIP ☑ Newark	c. LENGTH OF STAY (in this place) 86 years	c. CITY ☐ BOROUGH ☐ (Check box and give name) TOWNSHIP ☑ Newark	d. LENGTH OF STAY (in this place) 86 years

d. FULL NAME OF HOSPITAL OR INSTITUTION (If not in hospital or institution, give street address or location) 887 South 19th Street	e. STREET ADDRESS If rural, P. O. Address 887 South 19th Street

3. NAME OF DECEASED (Type or Print)	a. (First) Mary	b. (Middle)	c. (Last) Bruguier	4. DATE OF DEATH (Month) November 28, (Day) (Year) 1960

5. SEX Female	6. COLOR OR RACE White	7. MARRIED ☐ NEVER MARRIED ☐ WIDOWED ☑ DIVORCED ☐	8. DATE OF BIRTH May 15, 1874	9. AGE (In years last birthday) 86	If Under 1 Year Months Days 6	13	If Under 24 Hrs. Hours	Min.

10a. USUAL OCCUPATION (Give kind of work done during most of working life, even if retired) Housewife	10b. KIND OF BUSINESS OR INDUSTRY Home	11. BIRTHPLACE (State or foreign country) Newark, New Jersey	12. CITIZEN OF WHAT COUNTRY? U. S. A.

13. FATHER'S NAME Robert Feldweg	14. MOTHER'S MAIDEN NAME Unknown

15. WAS DECEASED EVER IN U.S. ARMED FORCES? (Yes, no, or unknown) (If yes, give war or dates of service) No	16. SOCIAL SECURITY NO. None 137-05-8612D	17. INFORMANT Mrs. Alma Rogers	Address I Meadowbrook Road Chatham, New Jersey

MEDICAL CERTIF.	20a. ACCIDENT ☐ SUICIDE ☐ HOMICIDE ☐ to the best of my knowledge.	20b. DESCRIBE HOW INJURY OCCURRED. (Enter nature of injury in Part I or Part II of item 10.)

20c. TIME OF INJURY	Hour a. m. p. m.	Month, Day, Year

20d. INJURY OCCURRED WHILE AT WORK ☐ NOT WHILE AT WORK ☐	20e. PLACE OF INJURY (e. g., in or about home, farm, factory, street, office bldg., etc.)	20f. CITY, TOWN, OR LOCATION	COUNTY	STATE

21. I attended the deceased from 7/12/60, to 11/28/60 and last saw her alive on 11/28/60. Death occurred at 1:05 p. m. on the date stated above; and to the best of my knowledge, from the causes stated.

22a. SIGNATURE Robert B J Mulvaney, M D	(Degree or title)	22b. ADDRESS 25 Longfellow Newark	22c. DATE SIGNED 11/29/60

23a. BURIAL, CREMATION, REMOVAL (Specify) Burial	23b. DATE 12/1/60	23c. NAME OF CEMETERY OR CREMATORY Fairmount Cemetery	23d. LOCATION (City, town or county) Newark	(State) New Jersey

24. FUNERAL DIRECTOR'S SIGNATURE HAEBERLE & BARTH	N.J. License No. 1385 & 1376	ADDRESS 571 CLINTON AVE. IRVINGTON 11, N. J.	25. DATE REC'D. BY LOCAL REG. 11/30/60	(Original Signed)

02/03/2000 NJ   STATE BUR OF VITAL STATISTICS

Page
73

SUZANNE'S BIRTH CERTIFICATE:

BIRTH RECORD, CARL FRIEDRICH ALEXANDER VON BRUGUIER

Many of the old German records require expert help to decipher completely, but for child 20, the names von Bruguier, Negendank, and Alexander Friedrich Karl were underlined by the minister or state official. This is from a military record at Frankfurt an den Oder, on the opposite side of the country from Jülich, where the letters said he was born. There is an entry for Oct. 29, 1814, when he was born, and another for December 7, when he was apparently baptized at Frankfurt an der Oder. It is interesting that the order of his names here is not the order of his names on the baptism records for his children, where it is given as Carl Friedrich Alexander. The letters were wrong about the exact birthplace of Francis and Emma von Bruguier, so perhaps they were wrong about the birth at Julich. Records do exist in the online parish registers in Julich for his brothers and sisters. This is from LDS Family History Center microfilm 0071206 of Kirchenbuch, 1723-1945, Evangelische Kirche, Frankfurt (Oder).

Newspaper notice about Francis Bruguier leaving Brandenburg without permission:

In German, but gives birth date, birth place, and last known residence:

(From the newspaper Königlich Preußischer Staats-Anzeiger, September 20, 1865, p. 3,026 in bound version) (Search for von Bruguier in books.google.de).

https://books.google.de/books?id=g4VNAAAAcAAJ&lpg=PA3026&ots=wjq2JM3LsM&dq=%22Von%20Bruguier%22&hl=de&pg=PA3026#v=onepage&q=%22Von%20Bruguier%22&f=false

"**Carl Ernst August von Bruguier aus Baerwaldt R./R., am 23 Mai 1841 zu Seeburg bei Spandau geboren,** evangelisch, ist auf Grund 110 des Strassgefessbuches und des Gesessed vom 10 Marz 1856 angeslagt, ohne Erlaubniss die Koniglichen Lande verlassen und sich dadurch dem Eintritt in den Dienst des Siebenden Heeres zu entziehen gesucht zu haben. Sur offentichen mundlichen Verhandlung uber diese Anlage ist auf den 29 November er, Vormittag 9 Uhr, an diesiger Gerichtsstelle im grossen Einungstaale Termin anberaumt. Der oben genannte ac von Bruguier wird aufgesorbert, in diesem Termine zur sestgestezten Stunde zu erscheinen und die zu seinter Bertheidigung dienenden Beweismittel mit zur Stelle zu bringen, ober solche uns so zeitig vor dem Termine anzuzeigen, dass sie noch zu demselben herbeigeschafft warden tonnen. Im Falle seines Ausbleibens wird mit der untersuchung und Entscheidung in contumaciam verfahren werden.

Custrin, den 3 August 1865.

Konigliches Kreisgericht I. Abtheilung."

The following report lists only seven generations of descendants of Johann von Bruguier. There have been a few generations after the seventh. It is possible that some individuals in the seventh generation are still living. In this report, plus sign indicates spouse.

Outline Descendant Report for JOHANN VON BRUGUIER

1 JOHANN VON BRUGUIER (- 1794) d: 20 Aug 1794 in near Milan,Italy

......2 CARL JOSEPH VON BRUGUIER (1786 - 1845) b: 29 Apr 1786, d: 28 Dec 1845 in Potsdam, Brandenburg, Germany

...... + ALBERTINE CAROLINA HENRIETTE NEGENDANK (1790 - 1844) b: 19 Jan 1790 in Berlin, Germany, m: Berlin, Germany, d: 10 Dec 1844 in Charlottenburg, Brandenburg, Germany

.........3 CARL FRIEDRICH ALEXANDER VON BRUGUIER (1814 - 1894) b: 29 Oct 1814 in Jülich, Rheinland, Germany, d: 08 Apr 1894

.... + SOPHIE HENRIETTE HERMINE KLEINHOLZ (1819 - 1900) b: 28 Jul 1819 in Altdöbern, Oberspreewald-Lausitz, Brandenburg, Germany, m: 1840, d: 06 Mar 1900

............4 CARL ERNST AUGUST FRANCIS VON BRUGUIER (1841 - 1906) b: 23 May 1841 in Seeburg, Potsdam-Mittelmark, Brandenburg, Germany; Per military record. Notice von Bruguiers were selling an estate in Seeburg in 1842., d: 24 Dec 1906 in Newark, Essex Co., New Jersey, USA

.... + ANNA WILHELMINE LADEWIG (1846 - 1915) b: 23 Aug 1846 in Brandenburg, Germany, m: 27 Feb 1866 in New York, New York, New York, USA, d: 08 Dec 1915 in Hamburg, Sussex Co., New Jersey, USA; ruptured appendix

...............5 Arthur Bruguier (about 1866 - about 1869) b: Abt. Jun 1866, d: Abt. 17 Dec 1869 in Newark, Essex Co, New Jersey, USA

...............5 Carl Frank E. Bruguier Jr (1870 - 1871) b: 30 Mar 1870 in New Jersey, d: 18 Jul 1871 in Newark, Essex Co., New Jersey, USA

...............5 Paul Charles Bruguier (1872 - 1934) b: 11 Oct 1872 in Newark, Essex Co, New Jersey, d: 20 May 1934 in Dover, Ocean Co., New Jersey

.... + Mary Boehm (1873 - 1942) b: 22 Jan 1873 in Newark, Essex Co., New Jersey, USA, m: 31 Mar 1896 in Newark, Essex Co., New Jersey, USA, d: 28 Jul 1942 in Middletown, Monmouth Co., New Jersey

...................6 Edna Mae Bruguier (1896 - 1956) b: 20 Aug 1896 in Newark, Essex County, New Jersey, USA, d: 12 Sep 1956 in Lakewood, Ocean, New Jersey, USA

.... + Victor R Lish (1894 - 1984) b: 1894 in New Jersey, m: 10 Sep 1915 in Newark, Essex Co., New Jersey, USA, d: 1984

.....................7 Edna Mae Lish (1916 - 1990) b: 12 May 1916 in New Jersey, d: 23 May 1990 in Riverside County, California

.....................7 Victor R Lish (1917 - 2015) b: 12 Aug 1917 in Newark, Essex County, New Jersey, USA, d: 21 Apr 2015 in Robbinsdale, Hennepin, Minnesota, USA

.... + Margaret Fitzpatrick

...................6 Wilhelmina Minerva Bruguier (1898 - 1984) b: 23 May 1898 in Newark, Essex, New Jersey, d: 21 Feb 1984 in Hollywood, Broward, Florida, USA

.... + Patrick Joseph Halloran (1895 - 1960) b: 26 Dec 1895 in Corofin, County Clare, Ireland, d: 17 Apr 1960

.....................7 Eleanor Halloran (about 1919 - before 2009) b: Abt. 1919 in New Jersey, d:Bef. Bef. 2009

.....................7 Katherine M. Halloran (1920 - 2008) b: 22 Apr 1920 in Columbiana, Ohio, United States, d: Jan 2008

.....................7 Winifred W Halloran (1920 - before 2008) b: 22 Apr 1920 in Columbiana, Ohio, United States, d: Bef. 2008

.....................7 Michael Halloran (1922 - before 2009) b: 09 Aug 1922 in Columbiana, Ohio, United States, d: Bef. 2009

.....................7 Lorraine Eileen Halloran (1928 - 2015) b: 10 Apr 1928 in Long Branch, Monmouth, New Jersey, USA, d: 18 Jan 2015 in Peachtree City, Fayette, Georgia, USA

.....................7 Patrick J. Halloran (about 1930 - before 2009) b: Abt. 1930 in New Jersey, d: Bef. 2009

.................6 Arthur A. Bruguier (1901 - 1979) b: 26 Jul 1901 in New Jersey, d: 04 Apr 1979 in Bristol, Connecticut

.... + Dorothy Koemmel (- 1932) m: 01 Apr 1925 in Manhattan, New York, USA, d: 1932

.....................7 George Arthur Bruguier (1929 - 2013) b: 29 Dec 1929 in Newark, Essex Co, New Jersey, USA, d: 14 Apr 2013 in St Cloud, Osceola, Florida, USA

.................6 Paul O. Bruguier (1903 - 2001) b: 22 Sep 1903 in New Jersey, d: 19 Mar 2001

.... + Elsa A. Shumacher (1908 - 1988) b: 1908, m: 03 Jul 1925 in Calvary Methodist Church, Keyport, N.J., d: 31 Dec 1988

..................6 Warren F. Bruguier (1906 - 1906) b: Jan 1906, d: 19 Mar 1906 in 57 Hamburg Pl.,
         Newark, New Jersey
..................6 Eleanor Maybell Bruguier (1907 - 1999) b: 09 May 1907 in 765 19th St., Newark,
         New Jersey, USA, d: 13 Oct 1999 in Linwood, Atlantic, New Jersey, USA
.... + Albert M. Jennings (1900 -) b: 1900 in New Jersey
..................7 Jeanne Edna Jennings (1931 - 2004) b: 16 Jan 1931 in Newark, Essex Co., New
         Jersey, USA, d: 25 Jan 2004 in Somers Point, New Jersey
..................6 Charles Roy Bruguier (1908 - 1969) b: 19 Dec 1908 in New Jersey, d: 18 Feb 1969
         in Edison, Middlesex, New Jersey, USA
.... + Leonore Ada Bell Burke (about 1917 -) b: Abt. 1917 in New Jersey, m: 08 Sep 1933 in
         Chestertown, Md.
..................7 Yvonne S. Bruguier (about 1936 - 1961) b: Abt. 1936 in New Jersey, d: 15 Nov 1961
         in Monmouth Co., New Jersey
.... + Dee Lennon (1922 - 1998) b: 11 Jun 1922 in Elizabeth Un, New Jersey, m: 31 Dec 1950,
         d: 25 Mar 1998 in Edison, Middlesex, New Jersey, USA
..................6 Lorraine D. Bruguier (1911 - 2003) b: 15 Dec 1911 in Newark Essex, New Jersey, d:
         24 Jan 2003 in Locust Grove, Orange, Virginia, USA
.... + William Rauch (about 1908 - before 2001) b: Abt. 1908 in New Jersey, d: Bef. 2001
..................6 Wilbur Bruguier (about 1917 - 1920) b: Abt. 1917 in New Jersey, d: 1920
...............5 OSCAR RICHARD BRUGUIER (1873 - 1950) b: 15 Dec 1873 in Newark, Essex Co., New
         Jersey, USA, d: 09 Oct 1950 in Newark, Essex Co., New Jersey, USA; Malignancy pylorus
.... + MARIE AUGUSTA FELDWEG (1874 - 1960) b: 15 May 1874 in Newark, Essex Co., New
         Jersey, USA, m: 20 May 1896 in Newark, Essex Co., New Jersey, USA, d: 28 Nov 1960 in
         Newark, Essex Co., New Jersey, USA
..................6 Alma Bertha Bruguier (1897 - 1989) b: 01 Apr 1897 in Newark, Essex Co., New
         Jersey, USA, d: 04 Oct 1989 in Weston, Fairfield, Connecticut, USA
.... + Percival A. Steinmuller Rogers (1893 - 1965) b: 1893 in Brooklyn, Kings Co., New York,
         USA, m: 23 Jun 1920, d: 21 Apr 1965 in Overlook Hospital, Summit, Union, New Jersey,
         USA
..................7 Geraldine Bruguier Rogers (1926 - 1994) b: 25 Dec 1926 in Newark Essex, New
         Jersey, d: 14 Apr 1994 in Greenwich, Fairfield, Connecticut; Age: 67 Years
.... + John Henry Glover III (1927 - 1999) b: 10 Jun 1927 in Orange, Essex, New Jersey,
         USA, m: 21 Jun 1952 in Madison, New Jersey, d: 07 Jan 1999
..................7 Blair Oakley Rogers (1923 - 2006) b: 14 Nov 1923 in Newark, Essex, New Jersey, USA,
         d: 05 Jan 2006 in Southampton, Suffolk, New York, USA; car accident in water
..................6 Lillian Mary Bruguier (1898 - 1966) b: 30 Aug 1898 in Newark, Essex Co., New
         Jersey, USA, d: 01 May 1966 in Richmond, Virginia, USA
.... + Eugene Masten Steenburgh (1895 - 1972) b: 25 Nov 1895 in Cohoes, Albany, New York,
         USA, m: 12 May 1920 in Newark, Essex Co, New Jersey, USA, d: 09 Feb 1972 in
         Richmond, Virginia, USA
..................7 Jeanne Audrey Steenburgh (1922 - after 2001) b: 26 Aug 1922 in Newark, Essex
         County, New Jersey, USA, d: Aft. Oct 2001
.... + Jack Theodore Kvernland (1917 - 1983) b: 12 Apr 1917 in Portland, Clackamas,
         Oregon, USA, m: 02 Jun 1945 in Newark, Essex Co, New Jersey, USA, d: 23 Sep 1983
         in Red Bank, Monmouth, New Jersey, USA
..................7 Donald Rae Steenburgh (1929 - 2001) b: 13 Feb 1929 in Newark, Essex, New Jersey,
         USA, d: 13 Oct 2001 in Montpelier, Hanover, Virginia, USA
.... + Lila Sutphin (about 1928 - after 2001) b: Abt. 1928, m: 19 Feb 1955 in Chesterfield,
         Virginia, USA, d: Aft. 2001

...............6 Irene Anna Bruguier (1900 - 2000) b: 04 Jan 1900 in Newark, Essex Co., New
 Jersey, USA, d: 04 Jul 2000 in Middletown, Newport, Rhode Island, USA
.... + Albert Everett Field (1899 - 1984) b: 21 Jan 1899 in Bronx,New York, m: 08 Oct 1924 in
 Newark, Essex Co, New Jersey, USA, d: 17 Aug 1984 in Lakewood, Ocean, New Jersey,
 USA
..............7 Richard Douglas Field (1928 - 2010) b: 16 Nov 1928 in New York, d: 03 Aug 2010
 in Manhasset, Nassau, New York, USA
..............7 Albert E Field, Jr. (1927 - 2013) b: 18 Mar 1927 in Richmond Hill, Queens, New York,
 USA, d: 10 Oct 2013
...............6 VIOLA ELIZABETH BERTHA BRUGUIER (1902 - 2000) b: 11 Nov 1902 in Newark,
 Essex Co., New Jersey, USA, d: 17 Sep 2000 in Lancaster, Pennsylvania, USA; natural
 causes
.... + HERBERT EUGENE DOWNS (1903 - 1982) b: 02 Apr 1903 in Newark, Essex Co., New
 Jersey, USA, m: 19 Mar 1926 in Newark, Essex Co., New Jersey, USA, d: 02 Apr 1982 in
 Boynton Beach, Palm Beach County, Florida, USA; emphysema
..............7 SUZANNE BRUGUIER DOWNS (1931 - 2014) b: 16 Jan 1931 in Newark, Essex
 Co., New Jersey, USA, m. 2 May 1953 in Bainbridge, Decatur, GA, d: 23 Apr 2014
 in Austin, Travis, Texas, USA
.... + JAMES JOSEPH KIRNER (1931 -) b: 15 Mar 1931 in Summit, Union, New Jersey,
 USA, m. 2 May 1953 in Bainbridge, Decatur, GA
.... + Albert Kirms (1906 - 1994) b: 30 Jul 1906 in Newark, Essex Co., New Jersey, USA, m:
 13 Aug 1967 in Bradley Beach, Monmouth, New Jersey, USA, d: 15 Oct 1994 in
 Monmouth, NJ, USA
..............7 Joyce Diane Downs (1933 - 2012) b: 07 Feb 1933 in Newark, Essex Co., New
 Jersey, USA, m. 17 Apr 1954 in Chatham, Morris, New Jersey, USA, d: 11 Feb 2012
 in Lancaster, Lancaster County, Pennsylvania, USA
.... + Carl Hahn Parker Jr. (1931 - 1995) b: 18 Oct 1931, d: 28 Jun 1995 in Lancaster,
 Pennsylvania, USA
...............6 Harold Oscar Bruguiere (1905 - 1954) b: 12 Jul 1905 in Newark, Essex, New Jersey,
 USA, d: 19 Oct 1954 in Berkeley Heights, Union, New Jersey, USA; cancer
.... + Altha Bunnell Smith (1908 - 1984) b: 1908 in New Jersey, d: 1984
..............7 Thomas Harold Bruguiere (1930 - 2014) b: 08 Apr 1930 in Paterson, Passaic,
 New Jersey, USA, d: 30 Sep 2014 in Nelson County, Virginia, USA
.... + Emilie Louise Dickie
..............7 Robert Smith Bruguiere
..............7 Jane Bruguiere
...............6 Oscar Robert Bruguiere (1908 - 1982) b: 23 Sep 1908 in Newark, Essex Co., New
 Jersey, USA, d: 27 May 1982 in Red Bank, Monmouth, New Jersey, USA; lung cancer
.... + Margaret Ruth Downs (1907 - 1999) b: 18 Mar 1907 in Newark, Essex Co., New Jersey,
 USA, m: 05 Oct 1930 in Newark, Essex Co., New Jersey, USA, d: 1999
..............7 Ronald Bruguiere
..............7 Peter Robert Bruguiere
...............6 Warren Kenneth Bruguiere (1911 - 1980) b: 16 Jul 1911 in Newark, Essex, New
 Jersey, USA, d: 14 May 1980 in Key Biscayne, Miami-dade, Florida, USA; Age: 68
.... + Edna Reuther (1911 - 2001) b: 17 Jan 1911 in Arlington, Hudson, New Jersey, USA, m:
 29 Nov 1935, d: 23 Nov 2001 in Worcester, MA.
..............7 Margot Mary Bruguiere (1939 - 2003) b: 08 Sep 1939 in Newark, Essex, New Jersey,
 USA, d: 13 Oct 2003 in Holden, Worcester County, Massachusetts, USA
.... + Robert James Martin Jr.
..............7 Christine Bruguier

.... + White

..................6 Laverne Audrey Bruguier (1918 - 1986) b: 23 Mar 1918 in Newark, Essex, New Jersey, USA, d: 10 Aug 1986 in Summit, Union, New Jersey, USA

.... + Ernest Everland Hancox Jr. (1913 - 1995) b: 17 Sep 1913, m: 06 Sep 1941 in Newark, Essex Co, New Jersey, USA, d: 24 Jul 1995 in Freehold, Monmouth, New Jersey, USA

....................7 Susan Lynne Hancox

.... + Charles Evans Trent

....................7 Robert Ernest Hancox

.... + Judy Hale

...............5 Richard F. BRUGUIER (1876 - 1876) b: 11 Jan 1876, d: 25 May 1876 in Newark, Essex Co, New Jersey, USA

...............5 Clara Hermine Bruguier (1879 - 1882) b: 26 Feb 1879 in Newark, Essex Co., New Jersey, USA, d: 12 Jan 1882 in Newark, Essex Co., New Jersey, USA;

...............5 Minnie Pauline Bruguier (1881 - 1977) b: 26 Jul 1881 in Newark, Essex Co., New Jersey, USA, d: Mar 1977 in Newton, Sussex Co., New Jersey, USA

.... + Marcus S. Henderson (1868 - 1924) b: 03 Jul 1868 in New Jersey, m: 26 Aug 1900 in Newfoundland, Morris County, New Jersey, USA, d: 08 Jul 1924

..................6 Clara A. Henderson (1902 - 1993) b: 22 Jul 1902 in New Jersey, d: 13 Jul 1993 in Hamburg, Sussex County, New Jersey, USA

.... + Roy Benjamin Casterlin (1899 - 1985) b: 24 Nov 1899 in New Jersey, d: 19 Jan 1985

..................6 Francis Bruguier Henderson (1905 - 1978) b: 23 Feb 1905 in New Jersey, d: Feb 1978 in Sussex, Sussex, New Jersey, USA

.... + Helen Shauger (1911 - 1978) b: 28 Mar 1911 in New Jersey, d: May 1978

....................7 Helen F Henderson

....................7 Kenneth M. Henderson (1932 - 2010) b: 09 Oct 1932 in Sussex, N.J, d: 06 Jun 2010 in Loveland, Larimer County, Colorado, USA

....................7 Willina P Henderson

....................7 Roy B Henderson

....................7 Francis Henderson (1943 - 1960) b: 1943, d: 1960

..................6 Beatrice E. Henderson (1908 - 1999) b: 28 May 1908 in Hamburg, New Jersey; 1910 census taken in May says she was 11 months old. Death record says born in 1908. Census more likely correct., d: 03 Jul 1999 in Avon, Hartford, Connecticut, USA

.... + Floyd C. Day (1905 - 1993) b: 11 Mar 1905 in New Jersey, d: 22 Nov 1993 in Hartford, Hartford, Connecticut, USA

....................7 Virginia V Day,(abt. 1929-?)

....................7 Helen M Day

....................7 Allen Day

..................6 Iona W. Henderson (1913 - 2003) b: 01 Jan 1913 in New Jersey, d: 11 Mar 2003 in Franklin, Sussex, New Jersey, USA

.... + Albert Havens Casterlin (about 1910 - 1947) b: Abt. 1910 in Sussex, Sussex County, New Jersey, USA, d: 31 Oct 1947 in Hamburg, Sussex County, New Jersey, USA

....................7 Clara Casterlin

....................7 Mahlon Roy Casterlin (1931 - 1989) b: 18 Jul 1931 in Hamburg Suss, New Jersey, d: 15 Jul 1989

....................7 Delores Casterlin

....................7 Reginald Dean Casterlin (about 1937 - 2012) b: Abt. 1937 in New Jersey, d: 26 May 2012

..................6 Kenneth M. Henderson

.... + Margaret Henderson (about 1919 -) b: Abt. 1919 in New Jersey

....................7 Kenneth M Henderson Jr.

....................7 Edward W Henderson

..................6 Marie Audrey Henderson (1921 - 1997) b: 05 Jul 1921 in Wantage Town, New Jersey, d: 01 Feb 1997 in Ogdensburg, Sussex, New Jersey, USA

.... + John Denike (about 1875 - 1933) b: Abt. 1875 in New Jersey, m: Abt. 1927, d: 29 Jan 1933 in Hamburg, Sussex Co., New Jersey, USA

.... + James E. Day (1872 - 1952) b: 1872 in New York, d: 05 Feb 1952 in Trenton, Mercer, New Jersey, USA

...............5 Franz Alexander Bruguier (1885 - 1885) b: Apr 1885 in Newark, Essex Co., New Jersey, USA, d: 15 Jul 1885 in Newark, Essex Co., New Jersey, USA

...............5 Male BRUGUIER (1887 - 1900) b: 11 Jun 1887 in Newark, Ward 6, Essex Co., N.J., d: 1900

...............5 Francis A. Bruguier Jr. (1888 - 1962) b: 11 Jun 1888 in Newark, Essex Co., New Jersey, USA, d: 09 Jul 1962 in Neptune City, Monmouth County, New Jersey, USA

.... + Mary H Berry (1893 - 1957) b: 01 Jul 1893 in Newark, Essex Co., New Jersey, USA, m: Sep 1910, d: 20 Jul 1957 in Keansburg, Monmouth, New Jersey, USA

..................6 Dorothy Mae Bruguier (1911 - 1973) b: 1911 in Newark, Essex, New Jersey, USA, d: 27 Apr 1973 in Neptune City, Monmouth County, New Jersey, USA

.... + Rudolph Fred Heinzinger (1909 - 1979) b: 20 Nov 1909 in California, USA, m: 08 Jun 1930 in Keansburg, Monmouth, New Jersey, USA, d: 22 Jun 1979 in Volusia, Florida, United States

.....................7 Dorothy Mae Heinzinger

.....................7 Rudolph F. Heinzinger, Jr.

.....................7 Richard Charles Heinzinger

.....................7 Ronald Frank Heinzinger

.....................7 Robert Heinzinger (before 1950 - before 1972) b: Bef. Sep 1950, d: Bef. 30 Apr 1972

.....................7 Heinzinger

..................6 Helen T. Bruguier (1912 - between 1972 and 2014) b: 1912 in New Jersey, d: Bet. 1972–2014

.... + Joseph H. Calver Jr. (1907 - 1961) b: 1907 in Bradevelt, Monmouth County, New Jersey, USA, d: 29 Dec 1961 in Long Branch, Monmouth County, New Jersey, USA

.....................7 Joseph Henry Calver (1933 - 2001) b: 13 Aug 1933 in Keansburg, Monmouth, New Jersey, USA, d: 30 Aug 2001 in Eatontown, Monmouth, New Jersey, USA

.....................7 Gary Richard Calver (1938 - 2014) b: 24 May 1938 in Red Bank, Monmouth, New Jersey, USA, d: 14 Jan 2014 in Anaheim, Orange, California, USA

.....................7 unknown Calver (about 1945 -) b: Abt. Dec 1945

..................6 Edmund Francis Bruguier (1915 - 1983) b: 25 Feb 1915 in New Jersey, USA, d: 21 Jun 1983 in Port Orange, Volusia, Florida, USA

.....................7 Sandra Josephine Bruguier

............4 Bertha Louise Agnes Emma von Bruguier (1843 - 1919) b: 14 May 1843 in Pritzen, Calau, Brandenburg, Germany, d: 18 Sep 1919

.... + Wilhelm Arlt (1837 - 1905) b: 30 Aug 1837 in Goschnitz, Silesia, m: 05 Nov 1867 in Bärwalde in Neumark, Germany, d: 10 Apr 1905

...............5 Meta Luisa Hermine Elisabeth Arlt (1868 - 1945) b: 25 Aug 1868, d: 1945

.... + Gustav Brühl (- after 1918) d: Aft. 1918

................6 Hildegard Brühl (1897 - 1897) b: 18 Jan 1897 in Berlin, Berlin, Deutschland, d: 20 Jan 1897 in Berlin, Berlin, Deutschland

................6 Gerda Brühl (- after 1962) d: Aft. 1962

..............5 Emma Berta Margarete Arlt (1870 -) b: 07 Jan 1870

..............5 Hans Arlt (1871 - 1941) b: 10 Jul 1871, d: 29 Dec 1941

..............5 Emma Arlt (1872 - 1874) b: 18 Dec 1872, d: 11 Dec 1874

..............5 Walda Arlt (1875 - 1877) b: 13 Jun 1875, d: 18 Jun 1877

..............5 Wilhelm Georg Arlt (1877 - 1878) b: 25 Jun 1877 in Stettin, Pomern, Germany, d: 08 Feb 1878

..............5 Erich Arlt (1878 - 1879) b: 04 Oct 1878, d: 29 May 1879

..............5 Willy Arlt (1880 - 1926) b: 01 Jul 1880, d: 19 Jun 1926

..............5 Meta Hulda Gertrude Arlt (1883 - after 1960) b: 15 Apr 1883, d: Aft. Oct 1960

..............5 Max Otto Erwin Arlt (1885 - after 1962) b: 14 Sep 1885 in Germany, d: Aft. Feb 1962

..........4 Friedrich Otto Eugen Rudolph von Bruguier (1844 - 1844) b: 14 May 1844 in Senftenberg,Germany, d: Oct 1844 in Senftenberg,Germany

..........4 Paul Bruguier (1845 - 1846) b: 22 Sep 1845 in Germany, d: 01 Jan 1846 in Germany

..........4 Friedrich Wilhelm Julius Otto von Bruguier (1857 - 1945 or 1946) b: 23 Jul 1857 in Germany, d: 1945 or 1946

.... + Anna Catharina Brehm (- 1929) m: 1895, d: 16 Apr 1929

..........4 Richard Bruguier (- 1856) b: Germany, d: 1856 in Germany

........3 Hugo Andreas Carl von Bruguier (1826 -) b: 11 Nov 1826 in Jülich, Rheinland, Germany

........3 Berta Maria Christina von Bruguier (1828 - 1896) b: 20 Aug 1828 in Jülich,Rheinland, Germany, d: 03 May 1896

........3 Otto Ludwig Friedrich Arnold Carl von Bruguier (1831 -) b: 15 Mar 1831 in Jülich, Rheinland, Germany

........3 Carl Emil Wilhelm Georg von Bruguier (1833 -) b: 16 Jul 1833 in Jülich, Rheinland, Germany

Source Title: **Birth Certificate, Downs, Herbert**

Repository: New Jersey State Bureau of Vital Statistics

Citation: State of New Jersey, Birth Certificate, Downs, Herbert (New Jersey State Dept. of Health and Senior Services), New Jersey State Bureau of Vital Statistics, Trenton, NJ.

DOWNS, HERBERT EUGENE, No. 17748

Source Title: **1870 United States Federal Census**

Repository: Ancestry.com

Citation: Ancestry.com, 1870 United States Federal Census (Provo, UT, USA, Ancestry.com Operations, Inc., 2009), Ancestry.com, Year: 1870; Census Place: Newark Ward 5, Essex, New Jersey; Roll: M593_880; Page: 488B; Image: 361; Family History Library Film: 552379.

VON BRUGUIER, CARL ERNST AUGUST FRANCIS

Source Title: **1880 United States Federal Census**

Repository: Ancestry.com

Citation: Ancestry.com and The Church of Jesus Christ of Latter-day Saints, 1880 United States Federal Census (Provo, UT, USA, Ancestry.com Operations Inc, 2010), Ancestry.com, Year: 1880; Census Place: Newark, Essex, New Jersey; Roll: 778; Family History Film: 1254778; Page: 540C; Enumeration District: 072; Image: 0742.

BRUGUIER, OSCAR RICHARD

Citation: Ancestry.com and The Church of Jesus Christ of Latter-day Saints, 1880 United States Federal Census (Provo, UT, USA, Ancestry.com Operations Inc, 2010), Ancestry.com, Year: 1880; Census Place: Newark, Essex, New Jersey; Roll: 778; Family History Film: 1254778; Page: 540C; Enumeration District: 072; Image: 0742.

Bruguier, Paul Charles

Citation: Ancestry.com and The Church of Jesus Christ of Latter-day Saints, 1880 United States Federal Census (Provo, UT, USA, Ancestry.com Operations Inc, 2010), Ancestry.com, Year: 1880; Census Place: Newark, Essex, New Jersey; Roll: 778; Family History Film: 1254778; Page: 540C; Enumeration District: 072; Image: 0742.

Bruguier, Clara Hermine

Citation: Ancestry.com and The Church of Jesus Christ of Latter-day Saints, 1880 United States Federal Census (Provo, UT, USA, Ancestry.com Operations Inc, 2010), Ancestry.com, Year: 1880; Census Place: Newark, Essex, New Jersey; Roll: 778; Family History Film: 1254778; Page: 540C; Enumeration District: 072; Image: 0742.

LADEWIG, ANNA WILHELMINE

Citation: Ancestry.com and The Church of Jesus Christ of Latter-day Saints, 1880 United States Federal Census (Provo, UT, USA, Ancestry.com Operations Inc, 2010), Ancestry.com, Year: 1880; Census Place: Newark, Essex, New Jersey; Roll: 778; Family History Film: 1254778; Page: 540C; Enumeration District: 072; Image: 0742.

VON BRUGUIER, CARL ERNST AUGUST FRANCIS

Source Title: **1880 United States Federal Census (con't)**

Repository: Ancestry.com

Citation: Ancestry.com and The Church of Jesus Christ of Latter-day Saints, 1880 United States Federal Census (Provo, UT, USA, Ancestry.com Operations Inc, 2010), Ancestry.com, Year: 1880; Census Place: Newark, Essex, New Jersey; Roll: 779; Family History Film: 1254779; Page: 85A; Enumeration District: 078; Image: 0170.

FELDWEG, MARIE AUGUSTA

Source Title: **1900 United States Federal Census**

Repository: Ancestry.com

Citation: Ancestry.com, 1900 United States Federal Census (Provo, UT, USA, Ancestry.com Operations Inc, 2004), Ancestry.com, Year: 1900; Census Place: Newark Ward 10, Essex, New Jersey; Roll: 965; Page: 3B; Enumeration District: 0099; FHL microfilm: 1240965.

Bruguier, Edna Mae

Citation: Ancestry.com, 1900 United States Federal Census (Provo, UT, USA, Ancestry.com Operations Inc, 2004), Ancestry.com, Year: 1900; Census Place: Newark Ward 10, Essex, New Jersey; Roll: 965; Page: 3B; Enumeration District: 0099; FHL microfilm: 1240965.

Boehm, Mary

Bruguier, Paul Charles

Citation: Ancestry.com, 1900 United States Federal Census (Provo, UT, USA, Ancestry.com Operations Inc, 2004), Ancestry.com, Year: 1900; Census Place: Newark Ward 10, Essex, New Jersey; Roll: 965; Page: 8B; Enumeration District: 0099; FHL microfilm: 1240965.

Bruguier, Minnie Pauline

Citation: Ancestry.com, 1900 United States Federal Census (Provo, UT, USA, Ancestry.com Operations Inc, 2004), Ancestry.com, Year: 1900; Census Place: Newark Ward 10, Essex, New Jersey; Roll: 965; Page: 8B; Enumeration District: 0099; FHL microfilm: 1240965.

Bruguier, Francis A. Jr

Citation: Ancestry.com, 1900 United States Federal Census (Provo, UT, USA, Ancestry.com Operations Inc, 2004), Ancestry.com, Year: 1900; Census Place: Newark Ward 10, Essex, New Jersey; Roll: 965; Page: 8B; Enumeration District: 0099; FHL microfilm: 1240965.

LADEWIG, ANNA WILHELMINE

Citation: Ancestry.com, 1900 United States Federal Census (Provo, UT, USA, Ancestry.com Operations Inc, 2004), Ancestry.com, Year: 1900; Census Place: Newark Ward 10, Essex, New Jersey; Roll: 965; Page: 8B; Enumeration District: 0099; FHL microfilm: 1240965.

VON BRUGUIER, CARL ERNST AUGUST FRANCIS

Citation: Ancestry.com, 1900 United States Federal Census (Provo, UT, USA, Ancestry.com Operations Inc, 2004), Ancestry.com, Year: 1900; Census Place: Newark Ward 12, Essex, New Jersey; Roll: 966; Page: 24B; Enumeration District: 0120; FHL microfilm: 1240966.

BRUGUIER, OSCAR RICHARD

FELDWEG, MARIE AUGUSTA

Citation: Ancestry.com, 1900 United States Federal Census (Provo, UT, USA, Ancestry.com Operations Inc, 2004), Ancestry.com, Year: 1900; Census Place: Newark Ward 12, Essex, New Jersey; Roll: 966; Page: 24B; Enumeration District: 0120; FHL microfilm: 1240966.

Bruguier, Alma Bertha

Citation: Ancestry.com, 1900 United States Federal Census (Provo, UT, USA, Ancestry.com Operations Inc, 2004), Ancestry.com, Year: 1900; Census Place: Newark Ward 12, Essex, New Jersey; Roll: 966; Page: 24B; Enumeration District: 0120; FHL microfilm: 1240966.

Bruguier, Lillian Mary

Citation: Ancestry.com, 1900 United States Federal Census (Provo, UT, USA, Ancestry.com Operations Inc, 2004), Ancestry.com, Year: 1900; Census Place: Newark Ward 12, Essex, New Jersey; Roll: 966; Page: 24B; Enumeration District: 0120; FHL microfilm: 1240966.

Bruguier, Irene Anna

Source Title: **1910 United States Federal Census**

Repository: Ancestry.com

Citation: Ancestry.com, 1910 United States Federal Census (Provo, UT, USA, Ancestry.com Operations Inc, 2006), Ancestry.com, Year: 1910; Census Place: Hardyston, Sussex, New Jersey; Roll: T624_909; Page: 18A; Enumeration District: 0173; FHL microfilm: 1374922.

Henderson, Clara A.

Citation: Ancestry.com, 1910 United States Federal Census (Provo, UT, USA, Ancestry.com Operations Inc, 2006), Ancestry.com, Year: 1910; Census Place: Hardyston, Sussex, New Jersey; Roll: T624_909; Page: 18A; Enumeration District: 0173; FHL microfilm: 1374922.

Henderson, Francis Bruguier

Citation: Ancestry.com, 1910 United States Federal Census (Provo, UT, USA, Ancestry.com Operations Inc, 2006), Ancestry.com, Year: 1910; Census Place: Hardyston, Sussex, New Jersey; Roll: T624_909; Page: 18A; Enumeration District: 0173; FHL microfilm: 1374922.

Henderson, Beatrice E.

Citation: Ancestry.com, 1910 United States Federal Census (Provo, UT, USA, Ancestry.com Operations Inc, 2006), Ancestry.com, Year: 1910; Census Place: Hardyston, Sussex, New Jersey; Roll: T624_909; Page: 18A; Enumeration District: 0173; FHL microfilm: 1374922.

Henderson, Marcus S.

Citation: Ancestry.com, 1910 United States Federal Census (Provo, UT, USA, Ancestry.com Operations Inc, 2006), Ancestry.com, Year: 1910; Census Place: Hardyston, Sussex, New Jersey; Roll: T624_909; Page: 18A; Enumeration District: 0173; FHL microfilm: 1374922.

Bruguier, Minnie Pauline

Citation: Ancestry.com, 1910 United States Federal Census (Provo, UT, USA, Ancestry.com Operations Inc, 2006), Ancestry.com, Year: 1910; Census Place: Newark Ward 10, Essex, New Jersey; Roll: T624_880; Page: 6A; Enumeration District: 0084; FHL microfilm: 1374893.

Bruguier, Harold Oscar

Citation: Ancestry.com, 1910 United States Federal Census (Provo, UT, USA, Ancestry.com Operations Inc, 2006), Ancestry.com, Year: 1910; Census Place: Newark Ward 10, Essex, New Jersey; Roll: T624_880; Page: 6A; Enumeration District: 0084; FHL microfilm: 1374893.

Bruguier, Lillian Mary

Citation: Ancestry.com, 1910 United States Federal Census (Provo, UT, USA, Ancestry.com Operations Inc, 2006), Ancestry.com, Year: 1910; Census Place: Newark Ward 10, Essex, New Jersey; Roll: T624_880; Page: 6A; Enumeration District: 0084; FHL microfilm: 1374893.

Bruguier, Irene Anna

Citation: Ancestry.com, 1910 United States Federal Census (Provo, UT, USA, Ancestry.com Operations Inc, 2006), Ancestry.com, Year: 1910; Census Place: Newark Ward 10, Essex, New Jersey; Roll: T624_880; Page: 6A; Enumeration District: 0084; FHL microfilm: 1374893.

BRUGUIER, OSCAR RICHARD

BRUGUIER, VIOLA ELIZABETH BERTHA

FELDWEG, MARIE AUGUSTA

Citation: Ancestry.com, 1910 United States Federal Census (Provo, UT, USA, Ancestry.com Operations Inc, 2006), Ancestry.com, Year: 1910; Census Place: Newark Ward 10, Essex, New Jersey; Roll: T624_880; Page: 6A; Enumeration District: 0084; FHL microfilm: 1374893.

Bruguier, Francis A. Jr.

Source Title: **1910 United States Federal Census (con't)**

Repository: Ancestry.com

Citation: Ancestry.com, 1910 United States Federal Census (Provo, UT, USA, Ancestry.com Operations Inc, 2006), Ancestry.com, Year: 1910; Census Place: Newark Ward 10, Essex, New Jersey; Roll: T624_880; Page: 6A; Enumeration District: 0084; FHL microfilm: 1374893.

LADEWIG, ANNA WILHELMINE

Citation: Ancestry.com, 1910 United States Federal Census (Provo, UT, USA, Ancestry.com Operations Inc, 2006), Ancestry.com, Year: 1910; Census Place: Newark Ward 16, Essex, New Jersey; Roll: T624_881; Page: 19A; Enumeration District: 0142; FHL microfilm: 1374894.

Bruguier, Edna Mae

Citation: Ancestry.com, 1910 United States Federal Census (Provo, UT, USA, Ancestry.com Operations Inc, 2006), Ancestry.com, Year: 1910; Census Place: Newark Ward 16, Essex, New Jersey; Roll: T624_881; Page: 19A; Enumeration District: 0142; FHL microfilm: 1374894.

Bruguier, Paul O.

Citation: Ancestry.com, 1910 United States Federal Census (Provo, UT, USA, Ancestry.com Operations Inc, 2006), Ancestry.com, Year: 1910; Census Place: Newark Ward 16, Essex, New Jersey; Roll: T624_881; Page: 19A; Enumeration District: 0142; FHL microfilm: 1374894.

Bruguier, Arthur A.

Citation: Ancestry.com, 1910 United States Federal Census (Provo, UT, USA, Ancestry.com Operations Inc, 2006), Ancestry.com, Year: 1910; Census Place: Newark Ward 16, Essex, New Jersey; Roll: T624_881; Page: 19A; Enumeration District: 0142; FHL microfilm: 1374894.

Bruguier, Wilhelmina Minerva

Citation: Ancestry.com, 1910 United States Federal Census (Provo, UT, USA, Ancestry.com Operations Inc, 2006), Ancestry.com, Year: 1910; Census Place: Newark Ward 16, Essex, New Jersey; Roll: T624_881; Page: 19A; Enumeration District: 0142; FHL microfilm: 1374894.

Bruguier, Charles Roy

Citation: Ancestry.com, 1910 United States Federal Census (Provo, UT, USA, Ancestry.com Operations Inc, 2006), Ancestry.com, Year: 1910; Census Place: Newark Ward 16, Essex, New Jersey; Roll: T624_881; Page: 19A; Enumeration District: 0142; FHL microfilm: 1374894.

Boehm, Mary

Citation: Ancestry.com, 1910 United States Federal Census (Provo, UT, USA, Ancestry.com Operations Inc, 2006), Ancestry.com, Year: 1910; Census Place: Newark Ward 16, Essex, New Jersey; Roll: T624_881; Page: 19A; Enumeration District: 0142; FHL microfilm: 1374894.

Bruguier, Paul Charles

Citation: Ancestry.com, 1910 United States Federal Census (Provo, UT, USA, Ancestry.com Operations Inc, 2006), Ancestry.com, Year: 1910; Census Place: Newark Ward 6, Essex, New Jersey; Roll: T624_878; Page: 3B; Enumeration District: 0045; FHL microfilm: 1374891.

DOWNS, HERBERT EUGENE

Source Title: **1920 United States Federal Census**

Repository: Ancestry.com

Citation: Ancestry.com, 1920 United States Federal Census (Provo, UT, USA, Ancestry.com Operations Inc, 2010), Ancestry.com, Year: 1920; Census Place: Hawthorne, Passaic, New Jersey.
Bruguier, Paul Charles

Ancestry.com, 1920 United States Federal Census (Provo, UT, USA, Ancestry.com Operations Inc, 2010), Ancestry.com, Year: 1920; Census Place: Hawthorne, Passaic, New Jersey; Roll: T625_1062; Page: 8A; Enumeration District: 15; Image: 740.

Bruguier, Lorraine D.

Citation: Ancestry.com, 1920 United States Federal Census (Provo, UT, USA, Ancestry.com Operations Inc, 2010), Ancestry.com, Year: 1920; Census Place: Hawthorne, Passaic, New Jersey; Roll: T625_1062; Page: 8A; Enumeration District: 15; Image: 740.

Bruguier, Eleanor Maybell

Citation: Ancestry.com, 1920 United States Federal Census (Provo, UT, USA, Ancestry.com Operations Inc, 2010), Ancestry.com, Year: 1920; Census Place: Hawthorne, Passaic, New Jersey; Roll: T625_1062; Page: 8A; Enumeration District: 15; Image: 740.

Bruguier, Paul O.

Citation: Ancestry.com, 1920 United States Federal Census (Provo, UT, USA, Ancestry.com Operations Inc, 2010), Ancestry.com, Year: 1920; Census Place: Hawthorne, Passaic, New Jersey; Roll: T625_1062; Page: 8A; Enumeration District: 15; Image: 740.

Bruguier, Arthur A.

Citation: Ancestry.com, 1920 United States Federal Census (Provo, UT, USA, Ancestry.com Operations Inc, 2010), Ancestry.com, Year: 1920; Census Place: Hawthorne, Passaic, New Jersey; Roll: T625_1062; Page: 8A; Enumeration District: 15; Image: 740.

Bruguier, Wilbur

Citation: Ancestry.com, 1920 United States Federal Census (Provo, UT, USA, Ancestry.com Operations Inc, 2010), Ancestry.com, Year: 1920; Census Place: Hawthorne, Passaic, New Jersey; Roll: T625_1062; Page: 8A; Enumeration District: 15; Image: 740.

Bruguier, Charles Roy

Citation: Ancestry.com, 1920 United States Federal Census (Provo, UT, USA, Ancestry.com Operations Inc, 2010), Ancestry.com, Year: 1920; Census Place: Hawthorne, Passaic, New Jersey; Roll: T625_1062; Page: 8A; Enumeration District: 15; Image: 740.

Boehm, Mary

Citation: Ancestry.com, 1920 United States Federal Census (Provo, UT, USA, Ancestry.com Operations Inc, 2010), Ancestry.com, Year: 1920; Census Place: Leetonia, Columbiana, Ohio; Roll: T625_1356; Page: 9A; Enumeration District: 137; Image: 331.

Halloran, Eleanor

Citation: Ancestry.com, 1920 United States Federal Census (Provo, UT, USA, Ancestry.com Operations Inc, 2010), Ancestry.com, Year: 1920; Census Place: Leetonia, Columbiana, Ohio; Roll: T625_1356; Page: 9A; Enumeration District: 137; Image: 331.

Halloran, Patrick Joseph

Citation: Ancestry.com, 1920 United States Federal Census (Provo, UT, USA, Ancestry.com Operations Inc, 2010), Ancestry.com, Year: 1920; Census Place: Leetonia, Columbiana, Ohio; Roll: T625_1356; Page: 9A; Enumeration District: 137; Image: 331.

Bruguier, Wilhelmina Minerva

Citation: Ancestry.com, 1920 United States Federal Census (Provo, UT, USA, Ancestry.com Operations Inc, 2010), Ancestry.com, Year: 1920; Census Place: Newark Ward 11, Essex, New Jersey; Roll: T625_1035; Page: 14A; Enumeration District: 223; Image: 1011.

DOWNS, HERBERT EUGENE

Citation: Ancestry.com, 1920 United States Federal Census (Provo, UT, USA, Ancestry.com Operations Inc, 2010), Ancestry.com, Year: 1920; Census Place: Newark Ward 16, Essex, New Jersey; Roll: T625_1038; Page: 10B; Enumeration District: 283; Image: 374.

Bruguier, Harold Oscar

Citation: Ancestry.com, 1920 United States Federal Census (Provo, UT, USA, Ancestry.com Operations Inc, 2010), Ancestry.com, Year: 1920; Census Place: Newark Ward 16, Essex, New Jersey; Roll: T625_1038; Page: 10B; Enumeration District: 283; Image: 374.

Bruguier, Alma Bertha

Citation: Ancestry.com, 1920 United States Federal Census (Provo, UT, USA, Ancestry.com Operations Inc, 2010), Ancestry.com, Year: 1920; Census Place: Newark Ward 16, Essex, New Jersey; Roll: T625_1038; Page: 10B; Enumeration District: 283; Image: 374.

Bruguier, Lillian Mary

Citation: Ancestry.com, 1920 United States Federal Census (Provo, UT, USA, Ancestry.com Operations Inc, 2010), Ancestry.com, Year: 1920; Census Place: Newark Ward 16, Essex, New Jersey; Roll: T625_1038; Page: 10B; Enumeration District: 283; Image: 374.

Bruguier, Irene Anna

Citation: Ancestry.com, 1920 United States Federal Census (Provo, UT, USA, Ancestry.com Operations Inc, 2010), Ancestry.com, Year: 1920; Census Place: Newark Ward 16, Essex, New Jersey; Roll: T625_1038; Page: 10B; Enumeration District: 283; Image: 374.

BRUGUIER, OSCAR RICHARD

BRUGUIER, VIOLA ELIZABETH BERTHA

FELDWEG, MARIE AUGUSTA

Citation: Ancestry.com, 1920 United States Federal Census (Provo, UT, USA, Ancestry.com Operations Inc, 2010), Ancestry.com, Year: 1920; Census Place: Newark Ward 6, Essex, New Jersey; Roll: T625_1033; Page: 10A; Enumeration District: 158; Image: 505.

Berry, Mary H.

Citation: Ancestry.com, 1920 United States Federal Census (Provo, UT, USA, Ancestry.com Operations Inc, 2010), Ancestry.com, Year: 1920; Census Place: Newark Ward 6, Essex, New Jersey; Roll: T625_1033; Page: 10A; Enumeration District: 158; Image: 505.

Bruguier, Helen T.

Citation: Ancestry.com, 1920 United States Federal Census (Provo, UT, USA, Ancestry.com Operations Inc, 2010), Ancestry.com, Year: 1920; Census Place: Newark Ward 6, Essex, New Jersey; Roll: T625_1033; Page: 10A; Enumeration District: 158; Image: 505.

Bruguier, Dorothy Mae

Citation: Ancestry.com, 1920 United States Federal Census (Provo, UT, USA, Ancestry.com
Operations Inc, 2010), Ancestry.com, Year: 1920; Census Place: Newark Ward 6,
Essex, New Jersey; Roll: T625_1033; Page: 10A; Enumeration District: 158; Image: 505.

Bruguier, Edmund Francis

Citation: Ancestry.com, 1920 United States Federal Census (Provo, UT, USA, Ancestry.com
Operations Inc, 2010), Ancestry.com, Year: 1920; Census Place: Newark Ward 6,
Essex, New Jersey; Roll: T625_1033; Page: 10A; Enumeration District: 158; Image: 505.

Bruguier, Francis A. Jr

Citation: Ancestry.com, 1920 United States Federal Census (Provo, UT, USA, Ancestry.com
Operations Inc, 2010), Ancestry.com, Year: 1920; Census Place: Wantage, Sussex,
New Jersey.

Bruguier, Minnie Pauline

Citation: Ancestry.com, 1920 United States Federal Census (Provo, UT, USA, Ancestry.com
Operations Inc, 2010), Ancestry.com, Year: 1920; Census Place: Wantage, Sussex,
New Jersey; Roll: T625_1068; Page: 9B; Enumeration District: 147; Image: 1147.

Henderson, Kenneth M.

Citation: Ancestry.com, 1920 United States Federal Census (Provo, UT, USA, Ancestry.com
Operations Inc, 2010), Ancestry.com, Year: 1920; Census Place: Wantage, Sussex,
New Jersey; Roll: T625_1068; Page: 9B; Enumeration District: 147; Image: 1147.

Henderson, Iona W.

Citation: Ancestry.com, 1920 United States Federal Census (Provo, UT, USA, Ancestry.com
Operations Inc, 2010), Ancestry.com, Year: 1920; Census Place: Wantage, Sussex,
New Jersey; Roll: T625_1068; Page: 9B; Enumeration District: 147; Image: 1147.

Henderson, Clara A.

Citation: Ancestry.com, 1920 United States Federal Census (Provo, UT, USA, Ancestry.com
Operations Inc, 2010), Ancestry.com, Year: 1920; Census Place: Wantage, Sussex,
New Jersey; Roll: T625_1068; Page: 9B; Enumeration District: 147; Image: 1147.

Henderson, Francis Bruguier

Citation: Ancestry.com, 1920 United States Federal Census (Provo, UT, USA, Ancestry.com
Operations Inc, 2010), Ancestry.com, Year: 1920; Census Place: Wantage, Sussex,
New Jersey; Roll: T625_1068; Page: 9B; Enumeration District: 147; Image: 1147.

Henderson, Beatrice E.

Citation: Ancestry.com, 1920 United States Federal Census (Provo, UT, USA, Ancestry.com
Operations Inc, 2010), Ancestry.com, Year: 1920; Census Place: Wantage, Sussex,
New Jersey; Roll: T625_1068; Page: 9B; Enumeration District: 147; Image: 1147.

Henderson, Marcus S.

Source Title: 1930 United States Federal Census

Repository: Ancestry.com

Citation: Ancestry.com, 1930 United States Federal Census (Provo, UT, USA, Ancestry.com Operations Inc, 2002), Ancestry.com, Year: 1930; Census Place: Franklin, Sussex, New Jersey; Roll: 1384; Page: 11B; Enumeration District: 0009; Image: 752.0; FHL microfilm: 2341119.

Shauger, Helen

Citation: Ancestry.com, 1930 United States Federal Census (Provo, UT, USA, Ancestry.com Operations Inc, 2002), Ancestry.com, Year: 1930; Census Place: Franklin, Sussex, New Jersey; Roll: 1384; Page: 11B; Enumeration District: 0009; Image: 752.0; FHL microfilm: 2341119.

Henderson, Francis Bruguier

Citation: Ancestry.com, 1930 United States Federal Census (Provo, UT, USA, Ancestry.com Operations Inc, 2002), Ancestry.com, Year: 1930; Census Place: Hamburg, Sussex, New Jersey; Roll: 1384; Page: 10B; Enumeration District: 0012; Image: 798.0; FHL microfilm: 2341119.

Casterlin, Roy B.

Citation: Ancestry.com, 1930 United States Federal Census (Provo, UT, USA, Ancestry.com Operations Inc, 2002), Ancestry.com, Year: 1930; Census Place: Hamburg, Sussex, New Jersey; Roll: 1384; Page: 10B; Enumeration District: 0012; Image: 798.0; FHL microfilm: 2341119.

Henderson, Clara A.

Citation: Ancestry.com, 1930 United States Federal Census (Provo, UT, USA, Ancestry.com Operations Inc, 2002), Ancestry.com, Year: 1930; Census Place: Hamburg, Sussex, New Jersey; Roll: 1384; Page: 12A; Enumeration District: 0012; Image: 801.0; FHL microfilm: 2341119.

Henderson, Kenneth M.

Citation: Ancestry.com, 1930 United States Federal Census (Provo, UT, USA, Ancestry.com Operations Inc, 2002), Ancestry.com, Year: 1930; Census Place: Hamburg, Sussex, New Jersey; Roll: 1384; Page: 12A; Enumeration District: 0012; Image: 801.0; FHL microfilm: 2341119.

Henderson, Marie Audrey

Citation: Ancestry.com, 1930 United States Federal Census (Provo, UT, USA, Ancestry.com Operations Inc, 2002), Ancestry.com, Year: 1930; Census Place: Hamburg, Sussex, New Jersey; Roll: 1384; Page: 12A; Enumeration District: 0012; Image: 801.0; FHL microfilm: 2341119.

Henderson, Iona W.

Citation: Ancestry.com, 1930 United States Federal Census (Provo, UT, USA, Ancestry.com Operations Inc, 2002), Ancestry.com, Year: 1930; Census Place: Hamburg, Sussex, New Jersey; Roll: 1384; Page: 12A; Enumeration District: 0012; Image: 801.0; FHL microfilm: 2341119.

Denike, John

Citation: Ancestry.com, 1930 United States Federal Census (Provo, UT, USA, Ancestry.com Operations Inc, 2002), Ancestry.com, Year: 1930; Census Place: Hamburg, Sussex, New Jersey; Roll: 1384; Page: 12A; Enumeration District: 0012; Image: 801.0; FHL microfilm: 2341119.

Bruguier, Minnie Pauline

Citation: Ancestry.com, 1930 United States Federal Census (Provo, UT, USA, Ancestry.com Operations Inc, 2002), Ancestry.com, Year: 1930; Census Place: Hamburg, Sussex, New Jersey; Roll: 1384; Page: 3A; Enumeration District: 0012; Image: 783.0; FHL microfilm: 2341119.

Day, Virginia V.

Citation: Ancestry.com, 1930 United States Federal Census (Provo, UT, USA, Ancestry.com Operations Inc, 2002), Ancestry.com, Year: 1930; Census Place: Hamburg, Sussex, New Jersey; Roll: 1384; Page: 3A; Enumeration District: 0012; Image: 783.0; FHL microfilm: 2341119.

Citation: Ancestry.com, 1930 United States Federal Census (Provo, UT, USA, Ancestry.com Operations Inc, 2002), Ancestry.com, Year: 1930; Census Place: Hamburg, Sussex, New Jersey; Roll: 1384; Page: 3A; Enumeration District: 0012; Image: 783.0; FHL microfilm: 2341119.

Day, Helen M

Citation: Ancestry.com, 1930 United States Federal Census (Provo, UT, USA, Ancestry.com Operations Inc, 2002), Ancestry.com, Year: 1930; Census Place: Hamburg, Sussex, New Jersey; Roll: 1384; Page: 3A; Enumeration District: 0012; Image: 783.0; FHL microfilm: 2341119.

Day, Floyd C.

Citation: Ancestry.com, 1930 United States Federal Census (Provo, UT, USA, Ancestry.com Operations Inc, 2002), Ancestry.com, Year: 1930; Census Place: Hamburg, Sussex, New Jersey; Roll: 1384; Page: 3A; Enumeration District: 0012; Image: 783.0; FHL microfilm: 2341119.

Henderson, Beatrice E.

Citation: Ancestry.com, 1930 United States Federal Census (Provo, UT, USA, Ancestry.com Operations Inc, 2002), Ancestry.com, Year: 1930; Census Place: Irvington, Essex, New Jersey; Roll: 1331; Page: 1B; Enumeration District: 0480; Image: 535.0; FHL microfilm: 2341066.

Rogers, Blair Oakley

Citation: Ancestry.com, 1930 United States Federal Census (Provo, UT, USA, Ancestry.com Operations Inc, 2002), Ancestry.com, Year: 1930; Census Place: Irvington, Essex, New Jersey; Roll: 1331; Page: 1B; Enumeration District: 0480; Image: 535.0; FHL microfilm: 2341066.

Bruguier, Alma Bertha

Citation: Ancestry.com, 1930 United States Federal Census (Provo, UT, USA, Ancestry.com Operations Inc, 2002), Ancestry.com, Year: 1930; Census Place: Irvington, Essex, New Jersey; Roll: 1331; Page: 1B; Enumeration District: 0480; Image: 535.0; FHL microfilm: 2341066.

Rogers, Geraldine Bruguier

Citation: Ancestry.com, 1930 United States Federal Census (Provo, UT, USA, Ancestry.com Operations Inc, 2002), Ancestry.com, Year: 1930; Census Place: Irvington, Essex, New Jersey; Roll: 1331; Page: 1B; Enumeration District: 0480; Image: 535.0; FHL microfilm: 2341066.

Rogers, Percival A. Steinmuller

Citation: Ancestry.com, 1930 United States Federal Census (Provo, UT, USA, Ancestry.com Operations Inc, 2002), Ancestry.com, Year: 1930; Census Place: Keansburg, Monmouth, New Jersey; Roll: 1371; Page: 7B; Enumeration District: 0050; Image: 92.0; FHL microfilm: 2341106.

Rauch, William

Citation: Ancestry.com, 1930 United States Federal Census (Provo, UT, USA, Ancestry.com Operations Inc, 2002), Ancestry.com, Year: 1930; Census Place: Keansburg, Monmouth, New Jersey; Roll: 1371; Page: 7B; Enumeration District: 0050; Image: 92.0; FHL microfilm: 2341106.

Bruguier, Lorraine D.

Citation: Ancestry.com, 1930 United States Federal Census (Provo, UT, USA, Ancestry.com Operations Inc, 2002), Ancestry.com, Year: 1930; Census Place: Keansburg, Monmouth, New Jersey; Roll: 1371; Page: 7B; Enumeration District: 0051; Image: 122.0; FHL microfilm: 2341106.

Heinzinger, Rudolph Fred

Citation: Ancestry.com, 1930 United States Federal Census (Provo, UT, USA, Ancestry.com Operations Inc, 2002), Ancestry.com, Year: 1930; Census Place: Keansburg, Monmouth, New Jersey; Roll: 1371; Page: 7B; Enumeration District: 0051; Image: 122.0; FHL microfilm: 2341106.

Citation: Ancestry.com, 1930 United States Federal Census (Provo, UT, USA, Ancestry.com
Operations Inc, 2002), Ancestry.com, Year: 1930; Census Place: Keansburg,
Monmouth, New Jersey; Roll: 1371; Page: 7B; Enumeration District: 0051; Image: 122.0;
FHL microfilm: 2341106.

Berry, Mary H
Citation: Ancestry.com, 1930 United States Federal Census (Provo, UT, USA, Ancestry.com
Operations Inc, 2002), Ancestry.com, Year: 1930; Census Place: Keansburg,
Monmouth, New Jersey; Roll: 1371; Page: 7B; Enumeration District: 0051; Image: 122.0;
FHL microfilm: 2341106.

Bruguier, Helen T
Citation: Ancestry.com, 1930 United States Federal Census (Provo, UT, USA, Ancestry.com
Operations Inc, 2002), Ancestry.com, Year: 1930; Census Place: Keansburg,
Monmouth, New Jersey; Roll: 1371; Page: 7B; Enumeration District: 0051; Image: 122.0;
FHL microfilm: 2341106.

Bruguier, Dorothy Mae
Citation: Ancestry.com, 1930 United States Federal Census (Provo, UT, USA, Ancestry.com
Operations Inc, 2002), Ancestry.com, Year: 1930; Census Place: Keansburg,
Monmouth, New Jersey; Roll: 1371; Page: 7B; Enumeration District: 0051; Image: 122.0;
FHL microfilm: 2341106.

Bruguier, Edmund Francis
Citation: Ancestry.com, 1930 United States Federal Census (Provo, UT, USA, Ancestry.com
Operations Inc, 2002), Ancestry.com, Year: 1930; Census Place: Keansburg,
Monmouth, New Jersey; Roll: 1371; Page: 7B; Enumeration District: 0051; Image: 122.0;
FHL microfilm: 2341106.

Bruguier, Francis A. Jr.
Citation: Ancestry.com, 1930 United States Federal Census (Provo, UT, USA, Ancestry.com
Operations Inc, 2002), Ancestry.com, Year: 1930; Census Place: Middletown,
Monmouth, New Jersey; Roll: 1371; Page: 6A; Enumeration District: 0076; Image: 340.0;
FHL microfilm: 2341106.

Halloran, Lorraine Eileen
Citation: Ancestry.com, 1930 United States Federal Census (Provo, UT, USA, Ancestry.com
Operations Inc, 2002), Ancestry.com, Year: 1930; Census Place: Middletown,
Monmouth, New Jersey; Roll: 1371; Page: 6A; Enumeration District: 0076; Image: 340.0;
FHL microfilm: 2341106.

Halloran, Winifred W
Citation: Ancestry.com, 1930 United States Federal Census (Provo, UT, USA, Ancestry.com
Operations Inc, 2002), Ancestry.com, Year: 1930; Census Place: Middletown,
Monmouth, New Jersey; Roll: 1371; Page: 6A; Enumeration District: 0076; Image: 340.0;
FHL microfilm: 2341106.

Halloran, Michael
Citation: Ancestry.com, 1930 United States Federal Census (Provo, UT, USA, Ancestry.com
Operations Inc, 2002), Ancestry.com, Year: 1930; Census Place: Middletown,
Monmouth, New Jersey; Roll: 1371; Page: 6A; Enumeration District: 0076; Image: 340.0;
FHL microfilm: 2341106.

Halloran, Katherine M.
Citation: Ancestry.com, 1930 United States Federal Census (Provo, UT, USA, Ancestry.com
Operations Inc, 2002), Ancestry.com, Year: 1930; Census Place: Middletown,
Monmouth, New Jersey; Roll: 1371; Page: 6A; Enumeration District: 0076; Image: 340.0;
FHL microfilm: 2341106.

Halloran, Patrick J.
Citation: Ancestry.com, 1930 United States Federal Census (Provo, UT, USA, Ancestry.com
Operations Inc, 2002), Ancestry.com, Year: 1930; Census Place: Middletown,
Monmouth, New Jersey; Roll: 1371; Page: 6A; Enumeration District: 0076; Image: 340.0;
FHL microfilm: 2341106.

Citation: Ancestry.com, 1930 United States Federal Census (Provo, UT, USA, Ancestry.com Operations Inc, 2002), Ancestry.com, Year: 1930; Census Place: Middletown, Monmouth, New Jersey; Roll: 1371; Page: 6A; Enumeration District: 0076; Image: 340.0; FHL microfilm: 2341106.

Halloran, Patrick Joseph

Citation: Ancestry.com, 1930 United States Federal Census (Provo, UT, USA, Ancestry.com Operations Inc, 2002), Ancestry.com, Year: 1930; Census Place: Middletown, Monmouth, New Jersey; Roll: 1371; Page: 6A; Enumeration District: 0076; Image: 340.0; FHL microfilm: 2341106.

Bruguier, Wilhelmina Minerva

Citation: Ancestry.com, 1930 United States Federal Census (Provo, UT, USA, Ancestry.com Operations Inc, 2002), Ancestry.com, Year: 1930; Census Place: Newark, Essex, New Jersey; Roll: 1336; Page: 1B; Enumeration District: 0104; Image: 3.0; FHL microfilm: 2341071.

Steenburgh, Jeanne Audrey

Citation: Ancestry.com, 1930 United States Federal Census (Provo, UT, USA, Ancestry.com Operations Inc, 2002), Ancestry.com, Year: 1930; Census Place: Newark, Essex, New Jersey; Roll: 1336; Page: 1B; Enumeration District: 0104; Image: 3.0; FHL microfilm: 2341071.

Steenburgh, Donald Rae

Citation: Ancestry.com, 1930 United States Federal Census (Provo, UT, USA, Ancestry.com Operations Inc, 2002), Ancestry.com, Year: 1930; Census Place: Newark, Essex, New Jersey; Roll: 1336; Page: 1B; Enumeration District: 0104; Image: 3.0; FHL microfilm: 2341071.

Steenburgh, Eugene Masten

Citation: Ancestry.com, 1930 United States Federal Census (Provo, UT, USA, Ancestry.com Operations Inc, 2002), Ancestry.com, Year: 1930; Census Place: Newark, Essex, New Jersey; Roll: 1336; Page: 1B; Enumeration District: 0104; Image: 3.0; FHL microfilm: 2341071.

Bruguier, Lillian Mary

Citation: Ancestry.com, 1930 United States Federal Census (Provo, UT, USA, Ancestry.com Operations Inc, 2002), Ancestry.com, Year: 1930; Census Place: Newark, Essex, New Jersey; Roll: 1338; Page: 10B; Enumeration District: 0175; Image: 668.0; FHL microfilm: 2341073.

Downs, Margaret Ruth

Citation: Ancestry.com, 1930 United States Federal Census (Provo, UT, USA, Ancestry.com Operations Inc, 2002), Ancestry.com, Year: 1930; Census Place: Newark, Essex, New Jersey; Roll: 1342; Page: 12B; Enumeration District: 0283; Image: 374.0; FHL microfilm: 2341077.

Bruguiere, Warren Kenneth

Citation: Ancestry.com, 1930 United States Federal Census (Provo, UT, USA, Ancestry.com Operations Inc, 2002), Ancestry.com, Year: 1930; Census Place: Newark, Essex, New Jersey; Roll: 1342; Page: 12B; Enumeration District: 0283; Image: 374.0; FHL microfilm: 2341077.

Bruguiere, Oscar Robert

Citation: Ancestry.com, 1930 United States Federal Census (Provo, UT, USA, Ancestry.com Operations Inc, 2002), Ancestry.com, Year: 1930; Census Place: Newark, Essex, New Jersey; Roll: 1342; Page: 12B; Enumeration District: 0283; Image: 374.0; FHL microfilm: 2341077.

Bruguier, Laverne Audrey

Citation: Ancestry.com, 1930 United States Federal Census (Provo, UT, USA, Ancestry.com Operations Inc, 2002), Ancestry.com, Year: 1930; Census Place: Newark, Essex, New Jersey; Roll: 1342; Page: 12B; Enumeration District: 0283; Image: 374.0; FHL microfilm: 2341077.

Citation: Ancestry.com, 1930 United States Federal Census (Provo, UT, USA, Ancestry.com Operations Inc, 2002), Ancestry.com, Year: 1930; Census Place: Newark, Essex, New Jersey; Roll: 1342; Page: 12B; Enumeration District: 0283; Image: 374.0; FHL microfilm: 2341077.

FELDWEG, MARIE AUGUSTA

Citation: Ancestry.com, 1930 United States Federal Census (Provo, UT, USA, Ancestry.com Operations Inc, 2002), Ancestry.com, Year: 1930; Census Place: Newark, Essex, New Jersey; Roll: 1342; Page: 12B; Enumeration District: 0283; Image: 374.0; FHL microfilm: 2341077.

BRUGUIER, OSCAR RICHARD

Citation: Ancestry.com, 1930 United States Federal Census (Provo, UT, USA, Ancestry.com Operations Inc, 2002), Ancestry.com, Year: 1930; Census Place: Nutley, Essex, New Jersey; Roll: 1344; Page: 12B; Enumeration District: 0565; Image: 346.0; FHL microfilm: 2341079.

Lish, Edna M

Citation: Ancestry.com, 1930 United States Federal Census (Provo, UT, USA, Ancestry.com Operations Inc, 2002), Ancestry.com, Year: 1930; Census Place: Nutley, Essex, New Jersey; Roll: 1344; Page: 12B; Enumeration District: 0565; Image: 346.0; FHL microfilm: 2341079.

Lish, Victor R

Citation: Ancestry.com, 1930 United States Federal Census (Provo, UT, USA, Ancestry.com Operations Inc, 2002), Ancestry.com, Year: 1930; Census Place: Nutley, Essex, New Jersey; Roll: 1344; Page: 12B; Enumeration District: 0565; Image: 346.0; FHL microfilm: 2341079.

Lish, Victor R

Citation: Ancestry.com, 1930 United States Federal Census (Provo, UT, USA, Ancestry.com Operations Inc, 2002), Ancestry.com, Year: 1930; Census Place: Nutley, Essex, New Jersey; Roll: 1344; Page: 12B; Enumeration District: 0565; Image: 346.0; FHL microfilm: 2341079.

Bruguier, Edna Mae

Citation: Ancestry.com, 1930 United States Federal Census (Provo, UT, USA, Ancestry.com Operations Inc, 2002), Ancestry.com, Year: 1930; Census Place: Queens, Queens, New York; Roll: 1598; Page: 18A; Enumeration District: 0356; Image: 505.0; FHL microfilm: 2341333.

Field, Albert E.

Citation: Ancestry.com, 1930 United States Federal Census (Provo, UT, USA, Ancestry.com Operations Inc, 2002), Ancestry.com, Year: 1930; Census Place: Queens, Queens, New York; Roll: 1598; Page: 18A; Enumeration District: 0356; Image: 505.0; FHL microfilm: 2341333.

Field, Albert Everett

Citation: Ancestry.com, 1930 United States Federal Census (Provo, UT, USA, Ancestry.com Operations Inc, 2002), Ancestry.com, Year: 1930; Census Place: Queens, Queens, New York; Roll: 1598; Page: 18A; Enumeration District: 0356; Image: 505.0; FHL microfilm: 2341333.

Field, Richard Douglas

Citation: Ancestry.com, 1930 United States Federal Census (Provo, UT, USA, Ancestry.com Operations Inc, 2002), Ancestry.com, Year: 1930; Census Place: Queens, Queens, New York; Roll: 1598; Page: 18A; Enumeration District: 0356; Image: 505.0; FHL microfilm: 2341333.

Bruguier, Irene Anna

Citation: Ancestry.com, 1930 United States Federal Census (Provo, UT, USA, Ancestry.com Operations Inc, 2002), Ancestry.com, Year: 1930; Census Place: Raritan, Monmouth, New Jersey; Roll: 1372; Page: 2B; Enumeration District: 98; Image: 684.0; FHL microfilm: 2341107.

Citation: Ancestry.com, 1930 United States Federal Census (Provo, UT, USA, Ancestry.com Operations Inc, 2002), Ancestry.com, Year: 1930; Census Place: Raritan, Monmouth, New Jersey; Roll: 1372; Page: 2B; Enumeration District: 98; Image: 684.0; FHL microfilm: 2341107.

Bruguier, Charles Roy

Citation: Ancestry.com, 1930 United States Federal Census (Provo, UT, USA, Ancestry.com Operations Inc, 2002), Ancestry.com, Year: 1930; Census Place: Raritan, Monmouth, New Jersey; Roll: 1372; Page: 2B; Enumeration District: 98; Image: 684.0; FHL microfilm: 2341107.

Boehm, Mary

Citation: Ancestry.com, 1930 United States Federal Census (Provo, UT, USA, Ancestry.com Operations Inc, 2002), Ancestry.com, Year: 1930; Census Place: Raritan, Monmouth, New Jersey; Roll: 1372; Page: 2B; Enumeration District: 98; Image: 684.0; FHL microfilm: 2341107.

Bruguier, Paul Charles

Source Title: **1940 United States Federal Census**

Repository: Ancestry.com

Citation: Ancestry.com, 1940 United States Federal Census (Provo, UT, USA, Ancestry.com Operations, Inc., 2012), Ancestry.com, Year: 1940; Census Place: Union, Union, New Jersey; Roll: T627_2390; Page: 63B; Enumeration District: 20-185. Record for Viola Downs B

.

BRUGUIER, VIOLA ELIZABETH BERTHA

Citation: Ancestry.com, 1940 United States Federal Census (Provo, UT, USA, Ancestry.com Operations, Inc., 2012), Ancestry.com, Year: 1940; Census Place: Chatham, Morris, New Jersey; Roll: T627_2370; Page: 8B; Enumeration District: 14-14.

KIRNER, JAMES JOSEPH

Citation: Ancestry.com, 1940 United States Federal Census (Provo, UT, USA, Ancestry.com Operations, Inc., 2012), Ancestry.com, Year: 1940; Census Place: Flower Hill, Nassau, New York; Roll: T627_2690; Page: 5B; Enumeration District: 30-215.

Field, Albert E

Citation: Ancestry.com, 1940 United States Federal Census (Provo, UT, USA, Ancestry.com Operations, Inc., 2012), Ancestry.com, Year: 1940; Census Place: Flower Hill, Nassau, New York; Roll: T627_2690; Page: 5B; Enumeration District: 30-215.

Field, Albert Everett

Citation: Ancestry.com, 1940 United States Federal Census (Provo, UT, USA, Ancestry.com Operations, Inc., 2012), Ancestry.com, Year: 1940; Census Place: Flower Hill, Nassau, New York; Roll: T627_2690; Page: 5B; Enumeration District: 30-215.

Field, Richard Douglas

Citation: Ancestry.com, 1940 United States Federal Census (Provo, UT, USA, Ancestry.com Operations, Inc., 2012), Ancestry.com, Year: 1940; Census Place: Flower Hill, Nassau, New York; Roll: T627_2690; Page: 5B; Enumeration District: 30-215.

Bruguier, Irene Anna

Citation: Ancestry.com, 1940 United States Federal Census (Provo, UT, USA, Ancestry.com
Operations, Inc., 2012), Ancestry.com, Year: 1940; Census Place: Hamburg, Sussex,
New Jersey; Roll: T627_2384; Page: 4B; Enumeration District: 19-12.

Casterlin, Roy B.

Citation: Ancestry.com, 1940 United States Federal Census (Provo, UT, USA, Ancestry.com
Operations, Inc., 2012), Ancestry.com, Year: 1940; Census Place: Hamburg, Sussex,
New Jersey; Roll: T627_2384; Page: 4B; Enumeration District: 19-12.

Henderson, Clara A.

Citation: Ancestry.com, 1940 United States Federal Census (Provo, UT, USA, Ancestry.com
Operations, Inc., 2012), Ancestry.com, Year: 1940; Census Place: Hartford, Hartford,
Connecticut; Roll: T627_537; Page: 7A; Enumeration District: 10-125.

Day, Virginia V.

Citation: Ancestry.com, 1940 United States Federal Census (Provo, UT, USA, Ancestry.com
Operations, Inc., 2012), Ancestry.com, Year: 1940; Census Place: Hartford, Hartford,
Connecticut; Roll: T627_537; Page: 7A; Enumeration District: 10-125.

Day, Helen M

Citation: Ancestry.com, 1940 United States Federal Census (Provo, UT, USA, Ancestry.com
Operations, Inc., 2012), Ancestry.com, Year: 1940; Census Place: Hartford, Hartford,
Connecticut; Roll: T627_537; Page: 7A; Enumeration District: 10-125.

Day, Floyd C.

Citation: Ancestry.com, 1940 United States Federal Census (Provo, UT, USA, Ancestry.com
Operations, Inc., 2012), Ancestry.com, Year: 1940; Census Place: Hartford, Hartford,
Connecticut; Roll: T627_537; Page: 7A; Enumeration District: 10-125.

Day, Allen

Citation: Ancestry.com, 1940 United States Federal Census (Provo, UT, USA, Ancestry.com
Operations, Inc., 2012), Ancestry.com, Year: 1940; Census Place: Hartford, Hartford,
Connecticut; Roll: T627_537; Page: 7A; Enumeration District: 10-125.

Henderson, Beatrice E.

Citation: Ancestry.com, 1940 United States Federal Census (Provo, UT, USA, Ancestry.com
Operations, Inc., 2012), Ancestry.com, Year: 1940; Census Place: Keansburg,
Monmouth, New Jersey; Roll: T627_2366; Page: 14B; Enumeration District: 13-56.

Berry, Mary H

Citation: Ancestry.com, 1940 United States Federal Census (Provo, UT, USA, Ancestry.com
Operations, Inc., 2012), Ancestry.com, Year: 1940; Census Place: Keansburg,
Monmouth, New Jersey; Roll: T627_2366; Page: 14B; Enumeration District: 13-56.

Bruguier, Francis A. Jr.

Citation: Ancestry.com, 1940 United States Federal Census (Provo, UT, USA, Ancestry.com
Operations, Inc., 2012), Ancestry.com, Year: 1940; Census Place: Keansburg,
Monmouth, New Jersey; Roll: T627_2366; Page: 17B; Enumeration District: 13-54.

Bruguier, Arthur A.

Citation: Ancestry.com, 1940 United States Federal Census (Provo, UT, USA, Ancestry.com
Operations, Inc., 2012), Ancestry.com, Year: 1940; Census Place: Keansburg,
Monmouth, New Jersey; Roll: T627_2366; Page: 17B; Enumeration District: 13-54.

Citation: Ancestry.com, 1940 United States Federal Census (Provo, UT, USA, Ancestry.com
Operations, Inc., 2012), Ancestry.com, Year: 1940; Census Place: Keansburg,
Monmouth, New Jersey; Roll: T627_2366; Page: 17B; Enumeration District: 13-54.

Bruguier, George Arthur

Citation: Ancestry.com, 1940 United States Federal Census (Provo, UT, USA, Ancestry.com
Operations, Inc., 2012), Ancestry.com, Year: 1940; Census Place: Keansburg,
Monmouth, New Jersey; Roll: T627_2366; Page: 17B; Enumeration District: 13-54.

Boehm, Mary

Citation: Ancestry.com, 1940 United States Federal Census (Provo, UT, USA, Ancestry.com
Operations, Inc., 2012), Ancestry.com, Year: 1940; Census Place: Keyport, Monmouth,
New Jersey; Roll: T627_2366; Page: 6B; Enumeration District: 13-62.

Burke, Leonore Ada Bell

Citation: Ancestry.com, 1940 United States Federal Census (Provo, UT, USA, Ancestry.com
Operations, Inc., 2012), Ancestry.com, Year: 1940; Census Place: Keyport, Monmouth,
New Jersey; Roll: T627_2366; Page: 6B; Enumeration District: 13-62.

Bruguier, Charles Roy

Citation: Ancestry.com, 1940 United States Federal Census (Provo, UT, USA, Ancestry.com
Operations, Inc., 2012), Ancestry.com, Year: 1940; Census Place: Keyport, Monmouth,

Bruguier, Yvonne S.

Citation: Ancestry.com, 1940 United States Federal Census (Provo, UT, USA, Ancestry.com
Operations, Inc., 2012), Ancestry.com, Year: 1940; Census Place: Long Branch,
Monmouth, New Jersey; Roll: T627_2367; Page: 61B; Enumeration District: 13-71.

Bruguiere, Warren Kenneth

Citation: Ancestry.com, 1940 United States Federal Census (Provo, UT, USA, Ancestry.com
Operations, Inc., 2012), Ancestry.com, Year: 1940; Census Place: Long Branch,
Monmouth, New Jersey; Roll: T627_2367; Page: 61B; Enumeration District: 13-71.

Reuther, Edna

Citation: Ancestry.com, 1940 United States Federal Census (Provo, UT, USA, Ancestry.com
Operations, Inc., 2012), Ancestry.com, Year: 1940; Census Place: Long Branch,
Monmouth, New Jersey; Roll: T627_2367; Page: 61B; Enumeration District: 13-71.

Bruguiere, Margot Mary

Citation: Ancestry.com, 1940 United States Federal Census (Provo, UT, USA, Ancestry.com
Operations, Inc., 2012), Ancestry.com, Year: 1940; Census Place: Middletown,
Monmouth, New Jersey; Roll: T627_2368; Page: 6B; Enumeration District: 13-111.

Bruguier, Eleanor Maybell

Citation: Ancestry.com, 1940 United States Federal Census (Provo, UT, USA, Ancestry.com
Operations, Inc., 2012), Ancestry.com, Year: 1940; Census Place: Middletown,
Monmouth, New Jersey; Roll: T627_2368; Page: 6B; Enumeration District: 13-111.

Jennings, Jeanne Edna

Citation: Ancestry.com, 1940 United States Federal Census (Provo, UT, USA, Ancestry.com
Operations, Inc., 2012), Ancestry.com, Year: 1940; Census Place: Middletown,
Monmouth, New Jersey; Roll: T627_2368; Page: 6B; Enumeration District: 13-111.

Citation: Ancestry.com, 1940 United States Federal Census (Provo, UT, USA, Ancestry.com
Operations, Inc., 2012), Ancestry.com, Year: 1940; Census Place: Middletown,
Monmouth, New Jersey; Roll: T627_2368; Page: 6B; Enumeration District: 13-111.

Jennings, Albert M.
Citation: Ancestry.com, 1940 United States Federal Census (Provo, UT, USA, Ancestry.com
Operations, Inc., 2012), Ancestry.com, Year: 1940; Census Place: Middletown,
Monmouth, New Jersey; Roll: T627_2368; Page: 9B; Enumeration District: 13-116.

Halloran, Lorraine Eileen
Citation: Ancestry.com, 1940 United States Federal Census (Provo, UT, USA, Ancestry.com
Operations, Inc., 2012), Ancestry.com, Year: 1940; Census Place: Middletown,
Monmouth, New Jersey; Roll: T627_2368; Page: 9B; Enumeration District: 13-116.

Halloran, Winifred W
Citation: Ancestry.com, 1940 United States Federal Census (Provo, UT, USA, Ancestry.com
Operations, Inc., 2012), Ancestry.com, Year: 1940; Census Place: Middletown,
Monmouth, New Jersey; Roll: T627_2368; Page: 9B; Enumeration District: 13-116.

Halloran, Michael
Citation: Ancestry.com, 1940 United States Federal Census (Provo, UT, USA, Ancestry.com
Operations, Inc., 2012), Ancestry.com, Year: 1940; Census Place: Middletown,
Monmouth, New Jersey; Roll: T627_2368; Page: 9B; Enumeration District: 13-116.

Halloran, Patrick Joseph
Citation: Ancestry.com, 1940 United States Federal Census (Provo, UT, USA, Ancestry.com
Operations, Inc., 2012), Ancestry.com, Year: 1940; Census Place: Middletown,
Monmouth, New Jersey; Roll: T627_2368; Page: 9B; Enumeration District: 13-116.

Bruguier, Wilhelmina Minerva
Citation: Ancestry.com, 1940 United States Federal Census (Provo, UT, USA, Ancestry.com
Operations, Inc., 2012), Ancestry.com, Year: 1940; Census Place: Neptune, Monmouth,
New Jersey; Roll: T627_2368; Page: 13A; Enumeration District: 13-135.

Heinzinger, Rudolph F., Jr.
Citation: Ancestry.com, 1940 United States Federal Census (Provo, UT, USA, Ancestry.com
Operations, Inc., 2012), Ancestry.com, Year: 1940; Census Place: Neptune, Monmouth,
New Jersey; Roll: T627_2368; Page: 13A; Enumeration District: 13-135.

Bruguier, Dorothy Mae
Citation: Ancestry.com, 1940 United States Federal Census (Provo, UT, USA, Ancestry.com
Operations, Inc., 2012), Ancestry.com, Year: 1940; Census Place: Neptune, Monmouth,
New Jersey; Roll: T627_2368; Page: 13A; Enumeration District: 13-135.

Heinzinger, Dorothy Mae
Citation: Ancestry.com, 1940 United States Federal Census (Provo, UT, USA, Ancestry.com
Operations, Inc., 2012), Ancestry.com, Year: 1940; Census Place: Neptune, Monmouth,
New Jersey; Roll: T627_2368; Page: 13A; Enumeration District: 13-135.

Heinzinger, Rudolph Fred
Citation: Ancestry.com, 1940 United States Federal Census (Provo, UT, USA, Ancestry.com
Operations, Inc., 2012), Ancestry.com, Year: 1940; Census Place: Newark, Essex, New
Jersey; Roll: T627_2427; Page: 3A; Enumeration District: 25-479.

Downs, Margaret Ruth
Citation: Ancestry.com, 1940 United States Federal Census (Provo, UT, USA, Ancestry.com
Operations, Inc., 2012), Ancestry.com, Year: 1940; Census Place: Newark, Essex, New
Jersey; Roll: T627_2427; Page: 3A; Enumeration District: 25-479.

Bruguiere, Oscar Robert
Citation: Ancestry.com, 1940 United States Federal Census (Provo, UT, USA, Ancestry.com
Operations, Inc., 2012), Ancestry.com, Year: 1940; Census Place: Newark, Essex, New
Jersey; Roll: T627_2427; Page: 3A; Enumeration District: 25-479.
Bruguier, Laverne Audrey

Ancestry.com, 1940 United States Federal Census (Provo, UT, USA, Ancestry.com Operations, Inc., 2012), Ancestry.com, Year: 1940; Census Place: Newark, Essex, New Jersey; Roll: T627_2427; Page: 3A; Enumeration District: 25-479.

Bruguiere, Ronald

Citation: Ancestry.com, 1940 United States Federal Census (Provo, UT, USA, Ancestry.com Operations, Inc., 2012), Ancestry.com, Year: 1940; Census Place: Newark, Essex, New Jersey; Roll: T627_2427; Page: 3A; Enumeration District: 25-479.

FELDWEG, MARIE AUGUSTA

Citation: Ancestry.com, 1940 United States Federal Census (Provo, UT, USA, Ancestry.com Operations, Inc., 2012), Ancestry.com, Year: 1940; Census Place: Newark, Essex, New Jersey; Roll: T627_2427; Page: 3A; Enumeration District: 25-479.

BRUGUIER, OSCAR RICHARD

Citation: Ancestry.com, 1940 United States Federal Census (Provo, UT, USA, Ancestry.com Operations, Inc., 2012), Ancestry.com, Year: 1940; Census Place: Nutley, Essex, New Jersey; Roll: T627_2338; Page: 8B; Enumeration District: 7-301.

Lish, Victor R

Citation: Ancestry.com, 1940 United States Federal Census (Provo, UT, USA, Ancestry.com Operations, Inc., 2012), Ancestry.com, Year: 1940; Census Place: Nutley, Essex, New Jersey; Roll: T627_2338; Page: 9A; Enumeration District: 7-301.

Lish, Edna M

Citation: Ancestry.com, 1940 United States Federal Census (Provo, UT, USA, Ancestry.com Operations, Inc., 2012), Ancestry.com, Year: 1940; Census Place: Nutley, Essex, New Jersey; Roll: T627_2338; Page: 9A; Enumeration District: 7-301.

Lish, Victor R

Citation: Ancestry.com, 1940 United States Federal Census (Provo, UT, USA, Ancestry.com Operations, Inc., 2012), Ancestry.com, Year: 1940; Census Place: Nutley, Essex, New Jersey; Roll: T627_2338; Page: 9A; Enumeration District: 7-301.

Bruguier, Edna Mae

Citation: Ancestry.com, 1940 United States Federal Census (Provo, UT, USA, Ancestry.com Operations, Inc., 2012), Ancestry.com, Year: 1940; Census Place: Ogdensburg, Sussex, New Jersey; Roll: T627_2384; Page: 6A; Enumeration District: 19-24.

Day, James E.

Citation: Ancestry.com, 1940 United States Federal Census (Provo, UT, USA, Ancestry.com Operations, Inc., 2012), Ancestry.com, Year: 1940; Census Place: Ogdensburg, Sussex, New Jersey; Roll: T627_2384; Page: 6A; Enumeration District: 19-24.

Bruguier, Minnie Pauline

Citation: Ancestry.com, 1940 United States Federal Census (Provo, UT, USA, Ancestry.com Operations, Inc., 2012), Ancestry.com, Year: 1940; Census Place: Philadelphia, Philadelphia, Pennsylvania; Roll: T627_3704; Page: 15A; Enumeration District: 51-564.

Parker, Carl Hahn Jr.

Citation: Ancestry.com, 1940 United States Federal Census (Provo, UT, USA, Ancestry.com Operations, Inc., 2012), Ancestry.com, Year: 1940; Census Place: Plainfield, Union, New Jersey; Roll: T627_2387; Page: 64B; Enumeration District: 20-66.

Bruguiere, Harold Oscar

Citation: Ancestry.com, 1940 United States Federal Census (Provo, UT, USA, Ancestry.com Operations, Inc., 2012), Ancestry.com, Year: 1940; Census Place: Plainfield, Union, New Jersey; Roll: T627_2387; Page: 64B; Enumeration District: 20-66.

Smith, Altha Bunnell

Citation: Ancestry.com, 1940 United States Federal Census (Provo, UT, USA, Ancestry.com Operations, Inc., 2012), Ancestry.com, Year: 1940; Census Place: Plainfield, Union, New Jersey; Roll: T627_2387; Page: 64B; Enumeration District: 20-66.

Bruguiere, Robert Smith

Citation: Ancestry.com, 1940 United States Federal Census (Provo, UT, USA, Ancestry.com Operations, Inc., 2012), Ancestry.com, Year: 1940; Census Place: Plainfield, Union, New Jersey; Roll: T627_2387; Page: 64B; Enumeration District: 20-66.

Bruguiere, Thomas Harold

Citation: Ancestry.com, 1940 United States Federal Census (Provo, UT, USA, Ancestry.com Operations, Inc., 2012), Ancestry.com, Year: 1940; Census Place: Red Bank, Monmouth, New Jersey; Roll: T627_2369; Page: 2B; Enumeration District: 13-154.

Calver, Joseph Henry

Citation: Ancestry.com, 1940 United States Federal Census (Provo, UT, USA, Ancestry.com Operations, Inc., 2012), Ancestry.com, Year: 1940; Census Place: Red Bank, Monmouth, New Jersey; Roll: T627_2369; Page: 2B; Enumeration District: 13-154.

Calver, Gary

Citation: Ancestry.com, 1940 United States Federal Census (Provo, UT, USA, Ancestry.com Operations, Inc., 2012), Ancestry.com, Year: 1940; Census Place: Red Bank, Monmouth, New Jersey; Roll: T627_2369; Page: 2B; Enumeration District: 13-154.

Bruguier, Helen T.

Citation: Ancestry.com, 1940 United States Federal Census (Provo, UT, USA, Ancestry.com Operations, Inc., 2012), Ancestry.com, Year: 1940; Census Place: Red Bank, Monmouth, New Jersey; Roll: T627_2369; Page: 2B; Enumeration District: 13-154.

Calver, Joseph H. Jr.

Citation: Ancestry.com, 1940 United States Federal Census (Provo, UT, USA, Ancestry.com
Operations, Inc., 2012), Ancestry.com, Year: 1940; Census Place: Union, Union, New
Jersey; Roll: T627_2390; Page: 63B; Enumeration District: 20-185.

DOWNS, HERBERT EUGENE

Citation: Ancestry.com, 1940 United States Federal Census (Provo, UT, USA, Ancestry.com
Operations, Inc., 2012), Ancestry.com, Year: 1940; Census Place: Union, Union, New
Jersey; Roll: T627_2390; Page: 63B; Enumeration District: 20-185.

Downs, Joyce Diane

Citation: Ancestry.com, 1940 United States Federal Census (Provo, UT, USA, Ancestry.com
Operations, Inc., 2012), Ancestry.com, Year: 1940; Census Place: Union, Union, New
Jersey; Roll: T627_2390; Page: 63B; Enumeration District: 20-185. Record for Suzanne
B. Downs.

DOWNS, SUZANNE BRUGUIER

Citation: Ancestry.com, 1940 United States Federal Census (Provo, UT, USA, Ancestry.com
Operations, Inc., 2012), Ancestry.com, Year: 1940; Census Place: Wantage, Sussex,
New Jersey; Roll: T627_2384; Page: 1B; Enumeration District: 19-36.

Henderson, Margaret

Citation: Ancestry.com, 1940 United States Federal Census (Provo, UT, USA, Ancestry.com
Operations, Inc., 2012), Ancestry.com, Year: 1940; Census Place: Wantage, Sussex,
New Jersey; Roll: T627_2384; Page: 1B; Enumeration District: 19-36.

Henderson, Kenneth M. Jr.

Citation: Ancestry.com, 1940 United States Federal Census (Provo, UT, USA, Ancestry.com
Operations, Inc., 2012), Ancestry.com, Year: 1940; Census Place: Wantage, Sussex,
New Jersey; Roll: T627_2384; Page: 1B; Enumeration District: 19-36.

Henderson, Edward W.

Citation: Ancestry.com, 1940 United States Federal Census (Provo, UT, USA, Ancestry.com
Operations, Inc., 2012), Ancestry.com, Year: 1940; Census Place: Wantage, Sussex,
New Jersey; Roll: T627_2384; Page: 1B; Enumeration District: 19-36.

Henderson, Willina P

Citation: Ancestry.com, 1940 United States Federal Census (Provo, UT, USA, Ancestry.com
Operations, Inc., 2012), Ancestry.com, Year: 1940; Census Place: Wantage, Sussex,
New Jersey; Roll: T627_2384; Page: 1B; Enumeration District: 19-36.

Henderson, Roy B.

Citation: Ancestry.com, 1940 United States Federal Census (Provo, UT, USA, Ancestry.com
Operations, Inc., 2012), Ancestry.com, Year: 1940; Census Place: Wantage, Sussex,
New Jersey; Roll: T627_2384; Page: 1B; Enumeration District: 19-36.

Henderson, Helen F.

Citation: Ancestry.com, 1940 United States Federal Census (Provo, UT, USA, Ancestry.com
Operations, Inc., 2012), Ancestry.com, Year: 1940; Census Place: Wantage, Sussex,
New Jersey; Roll: T627_2384; Page: 1B; Enumeration District: 19-36.

Citation: Ancestry.com, 1940 United States Federal Census (Provo, UT, USA, Ancestry.com
Operations, Inc., 2012), Ancestry.com, Year: 1940; Census Place: Wantage, Sussex,
New Jersey; Roll: T627_2384; Page: 1B; Enumeration District: 19-36.

Henderson, Kenneth M.

Citation: Ancestry.com, 1940 United States Federal Census (Provo, UT, USA, Ancestry.com
Operations, Inc., 2012), Ancestry.com, Year: 1940; Census Place: Wantage, Sussex,
New Jersey; Roll: T627_2384; Page: 1B; Enumeration District: 19-36.

Shauger, Helen

Citation: Ancestry.com, 1940 United States Federal Census (Provo, UT, USA, Ancestry.com
Operations, Inc., 2012), Ancestry.com, Year: 1940; Census Place: Wantage, Sussex,
New Jersey; Roll: T627_2384; Page: 1B; Enumeration District: 19-36.

Henderson, Kenneth M.

Citation: Ancestry.com, 1940 United States Federal Census (Provo, UT, USA, Ancestry.com
Operations, Inc., 2012), Ancestry.com, Year: 1940; Census Place: Wantage, Sussex,
New Jersey; Roll: T627_2384; Page: 1B; Enumeration District: 19-36.

Henderson, Francis Bruguier

Citation: Ancestry.com, 1940 United States Federal Census (Provo, UT, USA, Ancestry.com
Operations, Inc., 2012), Ancestry.com, Year: 1940; Census Place: Wantage, Sussex,
New Jersey; Roll: T627_2384; Page: 6A; Enumeration District: 19-36.

Casterlin, Clara

Citation: Ancestry.com, 1940 United States Federal Census (Provo, UT, USA, Ancestry.com
Operations, Inc., 2012), Ancestry.com, Year: 1940; Census Place: Wantage, Sussex,
New Jersey; Roll: T627_2384; Page: 6A; Enumeration District: 19-36.

Casterlin, Albert Havens

Citation: Ancestry.com, 1940 United States Federal Census (Provo, UT, USA, Ancestry.com
Operations, Inc., 2012), Ancestry.com, Year: 1940; Census Place: Wantage, Sussex,
New Jersey; Roll: T627_2384; Page: 6A; Enumeration District: 19-36.

Casterlin, Mahlon Roy

Citation: Ancestry.com, 1940 United States Federal Census (Provo, UT, USA, Ancestry.com
Operations, Inc., 2012), Ancestry.com, Year: 1940; Census Place: Wantage, Sussex,
New Jersey; Roll: T627_2384; Page: 6A; Enumeration District: 19-36.

Casterlin, Delores

Citation: Ancestry.com, 1940 United States Federal Census (Provo, UT, USA, Ancestry.com
Operations, Inc., 2012), Ancestry.com, Year: 1940; Census Place: Wantage, Sussex,
New Jersey; Roll: T627_2384; Page: 6A; Enumeration District: 19-36.

Casterlin, Reginald Dean

Citation: Ancestry.com, 1940 United States Federal Census (Provo, UT, USA, Ancestry.com
Operations, Inc., 2012), Ancestry.com, Year: 1940; Census Place: Wantage, Sussex,
New Jersey; Roll: T627_2384; Page: 6A; Enumeration District: 19-36.

Henderson, Iona W.

Source Title: **"Plainfield Slates Tribute for Milt", 2 Aug 1952, Page 27, The New York Age - at Newspapers.com**

Repository: www.newspapers.com

Citation: 2 Aug 1952, Page 27, The New York Age - at Newspapers.com, www.newspapers.com, www.newspapers.com.

http://www.newspapers.com/image/40475983/?terms=Harold%2BBruguiere.

Bruguiere, Harold Oscar

Source Title: **Berlin, Germany, Births, 1874-1899**

Repository: Ancestry.com

Citation: Ancestry.com, Berlin, Germany, Births, 1874-1899 (Provo, UT, USA, Ancestry.com Operations, Inc., 2015), Ancestry.com. 18 Jan 1897; Civil Registration Office Berlin IV b; certificate no. 155; archive sequence no. 37.

Citation: Brühl, Hildegard

Source Title: **Berlin, Germany, Selected Deaths, 1874-1920**

Repository: Ancestry.com

Citation: Ancestry.com, Berlin, Germany, Selected Deaths, 1874-1920 (Provo, UT, USA, Ancestry.com Operations, Inc., 2014), Ancestry.com. 20 Jan 1897; Civil Registration Office Berlin IV b; certificate no. 131; archive sequence no. 939.

Brühl, Hildegard

"Miss Margot Bruguiere is Married in Wellesley", Sep. 13, 1964, Section 4, p. 9, Boston Herald, Boston,

Source Title: **Massachusetts (online archive)**

Citation: *Boston Herald*, Boston, Massachusetts, online images (Genealogy Bank).

Bruguiere, Margot

Martin, Robert James Jr.

Source Title: **Brandenburg, Germany, Transcripts of Church Records, 1700-1874**

Repository: Ancestry.com

Citation: Ancestry.com, Brandenburg, Germany, Transcripts of Church Records, 1700-1874 (Provo, UT, USA, Ancestry.com Operations, Inc., 2011), Ancestry.com. 14 May 1843; Pritzen; Geburt; Vol. 337; Collection no. 5.

von Bruguier, Bertha Louise Agnes Emma

Source Title: **Bruguier family list of births and deaths**

Citation: Bruguier family list of births and deaths. Copy in possession of the author.

Arlt, Wilhelm

Bruguier, Francis A. Jr.

von Bruguier, Friedrich Wilhelm Julius Otto

Bruguier, Minnie Pauline

BRUGUIER, OSCAR RICHARD

Bruguier, Paul Charles

KLEINHOLZ, SOPHIE HENRIETTE HERMINE

LADEWIG, ANNA WILHELMINE

von Bruguier, Berta Maria Christina

von Bruguier, Bertha Louise Agnes Emma

Source Title: **Bruguier, Anna Ladewig Death Certificate**

Repository: New Jersey State Archives

Citation: State of New Jersey - Bureau of Vital Statistics, Bruguier, Anna Ladewig Death Certificate (Dec. 8, 1915), New Jersey State Archives, PO Box 307225 West State St. / Trenton, NJ 08625-0307 / 609-984-1050.; microfilm reel 404.

LADEWIG, ANNE WILHELMINE

Source Title: **Bruguier, Anna Pension File**

Repository: National Archives & Records Administration

Citation: Dept. of the Interior, Bureau of Pensions, Bruguier, Anna Pension File (Cert. 625614), National Archives & Records Administration.

LADEWIG, ANNA WILHELMINE

VON BRUGUIER, CARL ERNST AUGUST FRANCIS

Source Title: **Bruguier, Francis Death Certificate**

Repository: New Jersey State Bureau of Vital Statistics

Citation: Bureau of Vital Statistics, State of New Jersey, Bruguier, Francis Death Certificate, New
Jersey State Bureau of Vital Statistics, Trenton, NJ. 24 Dec. 1906.

VON BRUGUIER, CARL ERNST AUGUST FRANCIS

Source Title: **Bruguier, Mary death certificate**

Repository: New Jersey State Archives

Citation: State of NJ, Bruguier, Mary death certificate (28 Nov 1960), New Jersey State Archives,
PO Box 307225 West State St. / Trenton, NJ 08625-0307 / 609-984-1050. Cert. no. 48979.

FELDWEG, MARIE AUGUSTA

Source Title: **Bruguier, Oscar, Passport Application**

Bruguier, Oscar, Passport Application. National Archives and Records Administration (NARA);
Washington D.C.; Passport Applications, January 2, 1906 - March 31, 1925; Collection Number:
Citation: ARC Identifier 583830 / MLR Number A1 534; NARA Series: M1490; Roll #: 59. Issue date 29 Apr. 1908.

BRUGUIER, OSCAR RICHARD

Source Title: **Bruguier/Feldweg marriage certificate**

Repository: New Jersey State Archives

Citation: State of NJ, Bruguier/Feldweg marriage certificate (B-1777), New Jersey State Archives,
PO Box 307225 West State St. / Trenton, NJ 08625-0307 / 609-984-1050.

BRUGUIER, OSCAR RICHARD

FELDWEG, MARIE AUGUSTA

Source Title: **Bruguier/Ladewig Marriage Certificate**

Citation: Bruguier/Ladewig Marriage Certificate. Part of widow's pension (Cert. 625614).

LADEWIG, ANNA WILHELMINE

VON BRUGUIER, CARL ERNST AUGUST FRANCIS

Source Title: **California, Death Index, 1940-1997**

Repository: Ancestry.com

Citation: Ancestry.com, California, Death Index, 1940-1997 (Provo, UT, USA, Ancestry.com
Operations Inc, 2000), Ancestry.com, Date: 1990-05-23.

Lish, Edna M.

Source Title: **California, Divorce Index, 1966-1984**

Repository: Ancestry.com

Citation: Ancestry.com, California, Divorce Index, 1966-1984 (Provo, UT, USA, Ancestry.com
Operations Inc, 2007), Ancestry.com. Vol. K.

KIRNER, JAMES JOSEPH

Source Title: **Connecticut Death Index 1949-1996**

Citation: Connecticut Death Index 1949-1996. 4 Oct. 1989. State File no. 23157.

Bruguier, Alma Bertha

Source Title: **Connecticut Death Index, 1949-2001**

Repository: Ancestry.com

Citation: Connecticut Department of Health, Connecticut Death Index, 1949-2001 (Provo, UT,
USA, Ancestry.com Operations Inc, 2003), Ancestry.com.

Glover, John Henry III

Rogers, Geraldine Bruguier. 14 Apr. 1994. No. 08561

Source Title: **Connecticut Death Index, 1949-2012**

Repository: Ancestry.com

Citation: Connecticut Department of Health, Connecticut Death Index, 1949-2012 (Provo, UT, USA, Ancestry.com Operations, Inc., 2003), Ancestry.com. 4 Apr 1979. No. 06709.

Bruguier, Arthur A.

Citation: Connecticut Department of Health, Connecticut Death Index, 1949-2012 (Provo, UT, USA, Ancestry.com Operations, Inc., 2003), Ancestry.com. 4 Oct 1989. No. 23157.

Bruguier, Alma Bertha

Citation: Connecticut Department of Health, Connecticut Death Index, 1949-2012 (Provo, UT, USA, Ancestry.com Operations, Inc., 2003), Ancestry.com. 03 Jul 1999. No. 14774.

Henderson, Beatrice E.

Citation: Connecticut Department of Health, Connecticut Death Index, 1949-2012 (Provo, UT, USA, Ancestry.com Operations, Inc., 2003), Ancestry.com. 22 Nov 1993. No. 24501.

Day, Floyd C.

Source Title: **Death Certificate, Bruguier, Oscar**

Repository: New Jersey State Bureau of Vital Statistics

Citation: State Dept. of Health of New Jersey, Death Certificate, Bruguier, Oscar, New Jersey State Bureau of Vital Statistics, Trenton, NJ. 9 Oct 1950. No. 37293.

BRUGUIER, OSCAR RICHARD

Source Title: **Death Certificate, Herbert E. Downs**

Citation: Florida State Registrar's Office, Death Certificate, Herbert E. Downs (Florida Office of Vital Statistics). 2 Apr 1982. No. 82-035543.

DOWNS, HERBERT EUGENE

Source Title: **Downs/Bruguier marriage certificate**

Repository: New Jersey State Archives

Citation: State of NJ, Downs/Bruguier marriage certificate, New Jersey State Archives, PO Box 307225 West State St. / Trenton, NJ 08625-0307 / 609-984-1050. 19 Mar 1926. No. 664.

BRUGUIER, VIOLA ELIZABETH BERTHA
DOWNS, HERBERT EUGENE

Source Title: **Email from Ron Bruguiere dated 9/29/05**

Citation: Email from Ron Bruguiere dated 9/29/05.

Bruguiere, Oscar Robert
Downs, Margaret Ruth

Source Title: **Female Bruguier birth certificate**

Repository: New Jersey State Archives

Citation: State of NJ, Female Bruguier birth certificate (Nov. 11, 1902), New Jersey State Archives, PO Box 307225 West State St. / Trenton, NJ 08625-0307 / 609-984-1050. 11 Nov 1902. No. 25786.

BRUGUIER, VIOLA ELIZABETH BERTHA

Source Title: **Florida Death Index, 1877-1998**

Repository: Ancestry.com

Citation: Ancestry.com, Florida Death Index, 1877-1998 (Provo, UT, USA, Ancestry.com Operations Inc, 2004), Ancestry.com. 14 May 1980.

Bruguiere, Warren Kenneth

Source Title: **Florida Death Index, 1877-1998**

Repository: Ancestry.com

Citation: Ancestry.com, Florida Death Index, 1877-1998 (Provo, UT, USA, Ancestry.com Operations Inc, 2004), Ancestry.com. 21 Feb 1984.

Bruguier, Wilhelmina Minerva

Citation: Ancestry.com, Florida Death Index, 1877-1998 (Provo, UT, USA, Ancestry.com
Operations Inc, 2004), Ancestry.com. 21 Jun 1983.

Bruguier, Edmund Francis

Source Title: **Genealogy Bank obituary**

Repository: www.genealogybank.com

Citation: Genealogy Bank obituary (Richmond, VA, Richmond Times Dispatch, 3 May 1966),p. 24,
www.genealogybank.com.

Bruguier, Lillian Mary

Source Title: **Germany, Prussia, Brandenburg and Posen, Select Church Book Duplicates,**
1794-1874

Repository: Ancestry.com

Citation: Ancestry.com, Germany, Prussia, Brandenburg and Posen, Select Church Book
Duplicates, 1794-1874 (Provo, UT, USA, Ancestry.com Operations, Inc., 2014),
Ancestry.com. FHL Film 1334832. Vol. 337, 338, 1802-1874.

von Bruguier, Bertha Louise Agnes Emma

Citation: Ancestry.com, Germany, Prussia, Brandenburg and Posen, Select Church Book
Duplicates, 1794-1874 (Provo, UT, USA, Ancestry.com Operations, Inc., 2014),
Ancestry.com.

KLEINHOLZ, SOPHIE HENRIETTE HERMINE

Citation: Ancestry.com, Germany, Prussia, Brandenburg and Posen, Select Church Book
Duplicates, 1794-1874 (Provo, UT, USA, Ancestry.com Operations, Inc., 2014),
Ancestry.com.

VON BRUGUIER, CARL FRIEDRICH ALEXANDER

Citation: Ancestry.com, Germany, Prussia, Brandenburg and Posen, Select Church Book
Duplicates, 1794-1874 (Provo, UT, USA, Ancestry.com Operations, Inc., 2014),
Ancestry.com. FHL film 1273088. Vol. 317, 1816-1849.

von Bruguier, Friedrich Otto Eugen Rudolph

Source Title: **Germany, Select Births and Baptisms, 1558-1898**

Repository: Ancestry.com

Citation: Ancestry.com, Germany, Select Births and Baptisms, 1558-1898 (Provo, UT, USA,
Ancestry.com Operations, Inc., 2014), Ancestry.com. FHL film 297318. Vol. 20, p. 1500.

Arlt, Wilhelm

Citation: Ancestry.com, Germany, Select Births and Baptisms, 1558-1898 (Provo, UT, USA,
Ancestry.com Operations, Inc., 2014), Ancestry.com. FHL film 297318. Vol. 20, p. 1500.

von Bruguier, Bertha Louise Agnes Emma

Citation: Ancestry.com, Germany, Select Births and Baptisms, 1558-1898 (Provo, UT, USA,
Ancestry.com Operations, Inc., 2014), Ancestry.com. FHL film 297318. Vol. 20, p. 1500.

Arlt, Wilhelm Georg

Citation: Ancestry.com, Germany, Select Births and Baptisms, 1558-1898 (Provo, UT, USA,
Ancestry.com Operations, Inc., 2014), Ancestry.com. FHL film 920876. Ref. 2:1N4H18P.

von Bruguier, Carl Emil Wilhelm Georg

Citation: Ancestry.com, Germany, Select Births and Baptisms, 1558-1898 (Provo, UT, USA,
Ancestry.com Operations, Inc., 2014), Ancestry.com. FHL film 920876. Ref. 2:1N4H18P.

NEGENDANK, ALBERTINE CAROLINA HENRIETTE

Citation: Ancestry.com, Germany, Select Births and Baptisms, 1558-1898 (Provo, UT, USA,
Ancestry.com Operations, Inc., 2014), Ancestry.com. FHL film 920876. Ref. 2:1N4GJL7.

NEGENDANK, ALBERTINE CAROLINA HENRIETTE

Citation: Ancestry.com, Germany, Select Births and Baptisms, 1558-1898 (Provo, UT, USA,
Ancestry.com Operations, Inc., 2014), Ancestry.com. FHL film 920876. Ref. 2:1N4H18P.

VON BRUGUIER, CARL JOSEPH

Citation: Ancestry.com, Germany, Select Births and Baptisms, 1558-1898 (Provo, UT, USA,
Ancestry.com Operations, Inc., 2014), Ancestry.com.

Ancestry.com Operations, Inc., 2014), Ancestry.com. FHL film 920876. Ref. 2:1N4GJL7.

VON BRUGUIER, KARL JOSEPH

Citation: Ancestry.com, Germany, Select Births and Baptisms, 1558-1898 (Provo, UT, USA, Ancestry.com Operations, Inc., 2014), Ancestry.com. FHL film 920876. Ref. 2:1N4GJL7.

VON BRUGUIER, Otto Ludwig Friedrich Arnold Carl

Citation: Ancestry.com, Germany, Select Births and Baptisms, 1558-1898 (Provo, UT, USA, Ancestry.com Operations, Inc., 2014), Ancestry.com. FHL film 71206. 7 Dez. 1814.

VON BRUGUIER, CARL FRIEDRICH ALEXANDER

Citation: Ancestry.com, Germany, Select Births and Baptisms, 1558-1898 (Provo, UT, USA, Ancestry.com Operations, Inc., 2014), Ancestry.com. FHL film 71206. 7 Dez. 1814.

NEGENDANK, ALBERTINE CAROLINA HENRIETTE

Citation: Ancestry.com, Germany, Select Births and Baptisms, 1558-1898 (Provo, UT, USA, Ancestry.com Operations, Inc., 2014), Ancestry.com. FHL film 71206. 7 Dez. 1814.

VON BRUGUIER, KARL JOSEPH

Source Title: **Global, Find A Grave Index for Non-Burials, Burials at Sea, and other Select Burial Locations, 1300s-Current**

Repository: Ancestry.com

Citation: Ancestry.com, Global, Find A Grave Index for Non-Burials, Burials at Sea, and other Select Burial Locations, 1300s-Current (Provo, UT, USA, Ancestry.com Operations, Inc., 2012), Ancestry.com. 11 Feb 2012.

Downs, Joyce Diane

Citation: Ancestry.com, Global, Find A Grave Index for Non-Burials, Burials at Sea, and other Select Burial Locations, 1300s-Current (Provo, UT, USA, Ancestry.com Operations, Inc., 2012), Ancestry.com. 30 Sep 2014.

Bruguiere, Thomas Harold

Source Title: **Historical Newspapers, Birth, Marriage, & Death Announcements, 1851-2003**

Repository: Ancestry.com

Citation: Ancestry.com, Historical Newspapers, Birth, Marriage, & Death Announcements, 1851-2003 (Provo, UT, USA, Ancestry.com Operations Inc, 2006), Ancestry.com. "Jeanne Steenburgh will be wed.", N.Y. Times, 23 Dec 1944.

Steenburgh, Jeanne Audrey

Source Title: **Index to Death Records, June 1878 - June 1886, NJ**

Citation: Index to Death Records, June 1878 - June 1886, NJ (https://wwwnet1.state.nj.us/DOS/Admin/ArchivesDBPortal/DeathIndex.aspx).

Bruguier, Clara Hermine. 12 Jan 1882.

Bruguier, Franz Alexander 15 Jul 1885.

Source Title: **Jülich birth records**

Repository: LDS FHC Library

Citation: Deutschland Geburten und Taufen, 1558-1898," database, FamilySearch(https://familysearch.org/ark:/61903/1:1:VHSC-5VM:accessed 27 Nov 2015),Bertha Maria Christina von Bruguier, 21 Aug 1828; citing: FHL microfilm 920,876.

(https://familysearch.org/ark:/61903/1:1:VHSC-G6X:accessed 27 Nov 2015), Carl Emil Wilhelm Georg von Bruguier, 16 Jul 1833; citing: FHL microfilm 920,876.
(https://familysearch.org/ark:/61903/1:1:VHSC-235:accessed 27 Nov 2015), Hugo Andreas Carl von Bruguier, 12 Nov 1826; citing: FHL microfilm 920,875.
(https://familysearch.org/ark:/61903/1:1:VHSC-GRT:accessed 27 Nov 2015), Otto Ludwig Friederich Arnold Carl von Bruguier, 16 Mar 1831; citing: FHL microfilm 920,876.

Source Title: Letter describing Bruguier family Bible entries (in Germany)

Citation: Gerda Arlt, Letter describing Bruguier family Bible entries (in Germany). Copy in possession of the author.

Arlt, Emma

Arlt, Emma Berta Margarete

Arlt, Erich

Arlt, Hans

Arlt, Max Otto Erwin

Arlt, Meta Hulda Gertrude

Arlt, Walda

Arlt, Wilhelm

Arlt, Wilhelm Georg

Arlt, Willy

Brehm, Anna Catharina

von Bruguier, Friedrich Wilhelm Julius Otto

Bruguier, Paul

KLEINHOLZ, SOPHIE HENRIETTE HERMINE

NEGENDANK, ALBERTINE CAROLINA HENRIETTE

von Bruguier, Berta Maria Christina

von Bruguier, Bertha Louise Agnes Emma

VON BRUGUIER, CARL ERNST AUGUST FRANCIS

von Bruguier, Friedrich Otto Eugen Rudolph

VON BRUGUIER, JOHANN

VON BRUGUIER, CARL FRIEDRICH ALEXANDER

VON BRUGUIER, KARL JOSEPH

Source Title: Massachusetts, Town and Vital Records, 1620-1988

Repository: Ancestry.com

Citation: Ancestry.com, Massachusetts, Town and Vital Records, 1620-1988 (Provo, UT, USA, Ancestry.com Operations, Inc., 2011), Ancestry.com. [Source citation includes media item(s)]. "Marriages Registered in the Town of Edgartown, 1965", p. 161.

Bruguiere, Robert Smith

Citation: Hoglund, Judith Ann

Source Title: **New Jersey, Births and Christenings Index, 1660-1931**

Repository: Ancestry.com

Citation: Ancestry.com, New Jersey, Births and Christenings Index, 1660-1931 (Provo, UT, USA, Ancestry.com Operations, Inc., 2011), Ancestry.com. 30 Aug 1898. FHL Film No. 494240.

Bruguier, Lillian Mary

BRUGUIER, OSCAR RICHARD

FELDWEG, MARIE AUGUSTA

Citation: Ancestry.com, New Jersey, Births and Christenings Index, 1660-1931 (Provo, UT, USA, Ancestry.com Operations, Inc., 2011), Ancestry.com. 1 Jul 1893. FHL Film No. 494225.

Berry, Mary H

Citation: Ancestry.com, New Jersey, Births and Christenings Index, 1660-1931 (Provo, UT, USA, Ancestry.com Operations, Inc., 2011), Ancestry.com. 23 May 1898. FHL Film No. 494240.

Bruguier, Wilhelmina Minerva

Citation: Ancestry.com, New Jersey, Births and Christenings Index, 1660-1931 (Provo, UT, USA, Ancestry.com Operations, Inc., 2011), Ancestry.com. 11 Jun 1887. FHL Film No. 494207.

Bruguier, Francis A. Jr..

Citation: Ancestry.com, New Jersey, Births and Christenings Index, 1660-1931 (Provo, UT, USA, Ancestry.com Operations, Inc., 2011), Ancestry.com. 26 Jul 1881. FHL Film No. 494193.

Bruguier, Minnie Pauline

Source Title: **New Jersey, Compiled Census and Census Substitutes Index, 1643-1890**

Repository: Ancestry.com

Citation: Ancestry.com, New Jersey, Compiled Census and Census Substitutes Index, 1643-1890 (Provo, UT, USA, Ancestry.com Operations Inc, 1999), Ancestry.com. N.J. 1890 Veterans' Schedules. ED 216 Newark, Essex Co. p. 002.

VON BRUGUIER, CARL ERNST AUGUST FRANCIS

Source Title: **New Jersey, Deaths and Burials Index, 1798-1971**

Repository: Ancestry.com

Citation: Ancestry.com, New Jersey, Deaths and Burials Index, 1798-1971 (Provo, UT, USA, Ancestry.com Operations, Inc., 2011), Ancestry.com. 18 Jul 1871. FHL Film No. 584592.

Bruguier, Carl Frank E. Jr

Citation: Ancestry.com, New Jersey, Deaths and Burials Index, 1798-1971 (Provo, UT, USA, Ancestry.com Operations, Inc., 2011), Ancestry.com. 12 Jan 1882. FHL Film No. 589833.

Bruguier, Clara Hermine

Citation: Ancestry.com, New Jersey, Deaths and Burials Index, 1798-1971 (Provo, UT, USA, Ancestry.com Operations, Inc., 2011), Ancestry.com. 25 May 1876. FHL Film No. 584600.

BRUGUIER, Richard F.

Source Title: **New Jersey, Marriages, 1678-1985, index**

Citation: New Jersey, Marriages, 1678-1985, index, LDS Film 589822. Reference ID: p119rn26.

Bruguier, Minnie Pauline

Henderson, Marcus S.

Source Title: **New Jersey, State Census, 1895**

Repository: Ancestry.com

Citation: Ancestry.com, New Jersey, State Census, 1895 (Provo, UT, USA, Ancestry.com Operations Inc, 2007), Ancestry.com. Essex Co., Newark Ward 10, Family 54, Roll V227_71,p. 9, line 2.

VON BRUGUIER, CARL ERNST AUGUST FRANCIS

Source Title: **Geraldine B. Rogers New York Times article**

"Geraldine B. Rogers Lists 5 Attendants", New York Times, 29 May 1952, p. 18. Query.nytimes.com, accessed 28 Nov.

Citation: 2015.

Glover, John Henry III

Rogers, Geraldine Bruguier

Source Title: **New York, Petitions for Naturalization, 1794-1906**

Repository: Ancestry.com

Citation: Ancestry.com, New York, Petitions for Naturalization, 1794-1906 (Provo, UT, USA, Ancestry.com Operations, Inc., 2013), Ancestry.com. 10 Jul 1865. City Court Brooklyn (1-65), p. 186.

VON BRUGUIER, CARL ERNST AUGUST FRANCIS

Source Title: **New York, New York, Marriage Indexes 1866-1937**

Repository: Ancestry.com

Citation: Ancestry.com, New York, New York, Marriage Indexes 1866-1937 (Provo, UT, USA, Ancestry.com Operations, Inc., 2014), Ancestry.com. 1 Apr 1925. Manhattan. Certificate no. 10602.

Bruguier, Arthur A.

Citation: Koemmel, Dorothy

Source Title: **New York, Passenger Lists, 1820-1957**

Repository: Ancestry.com

Citation: Ancestry.com, New York, Passenger Lists, 1820-1957 (Provo, UT, USA, Ancestry.com Operations, Inc., 2010), Ancestry.com, Year: 1862. Image 398. 26 Jun 1862. M237, roll 220, Coriolan, line 142.

VON BRUGUIER, CARL ERNST AUGUST FRANCIS

Citation: Ancestry.com, New York, Passenger Lists, 1820-1957 (Provo, UT, USA, Ancestry.com Operations, Inc., 2010), Ancestry.com, Year: 1908; Arrival: New York, New York; Microfilm Serial: T715, 1897-1957; Microfilm Roll: Roll 1124; Line: 28; Page Number: 93.

BRUGUIER, OSCAR RICHARD

Citation: Ancestry.com, New York, Passenger Lists, 1820-1957 (Provo, UT, USA, Ancestry.com Operations, Inc., 2010), Ancestry.com, Year: 1935; Arrival: New York, New York; Microfilm Serial: T715, 1897-1957; Microfilm Roll: Roll 5739; Line: 1; Page Number: 180.

Bruguiere, Warren Kenneth

Source Title: **Newark Evening News Deaths Notices 24 Dec. 1906.**

Repository: New Jersey State Archives

Citation: Newark Evening News. 24 Dec 1906. P. 12. Col. 1.

LADEWIG, ANNA WILHELMINE

VON BRUGUIER, CARL ERNST AUGUST FRANCIS

Source Title: **Newark, New Jersey Directory, 1890-91**

Repository: Ancestry.com

Citation: Ancestry.com, Newark, New Jersey Directory, 1890-91 (Provo, UT, USA, Ancestry.com Operations Inc, 2000), Ancestry.com.

VON BRUGUIER, CARL ERNST AUGUST FRANCIS

Source Title: **Obit, Calver, Gary Richard**

Repository: GenealogyBank.com

Citation: Orange County Register, The (Santa Ana, CA), Obit, Calver, Gary Richard, 26 Jan 2014), GenealogyBank.com(http://www.genealogybank.com/doc/obituaries/obit/14B998D53A292CE8-14B998D53A292CE8 : accessed 29 November 2015)

Source Title: **Ohio, Birth Index, 1908-1964**

Repository: Ancestry.com

Citation: Ancestry.com, Ohio, Birth Index, 1908-1964 (Provo, UT, USA, Ancestry.com Operations, Inc., 2012), Ancestry.com. 22 Apr 1920. State File no. 1920038878.

Halloran, Winifred W

Citation: Ancestry.com, Ohio, Birth Index, 1908-1964 (Provo, UT, USA, Ancestry.com Operations, Inc., 2012), Ancestry.com. 9 Aug 1922. State File no. 1922070893.

Halloran, Michael

Citation: Ancestry.com, Ohio, Birth Index, 1908-1964 (Provo, UT, USA, Ancestry.com Operations, Inc., 2012), Ancestry.com. 22 Apr 1920. State File no. 1920038879.

Halloran, Katherine M.

Source Title: **Passenger lists 21 July 1855 - 22 Aug 1855, New York City**

Repository: LDS FHC Library

Citation: Passenger lists 21 July 1855 - 22 Aug 1855, New York City (Microfilm # 175511), LDS FHC Library, Salt Lake City, Utah. 27 Jul 1855, Ship Herschel.

LADEWIG, ANNA WILHELMINE

Source Title: **Passenger Ships and Images**

Repository: Ancestry.com

Citation: Ancestry.com, Passenger Ships and Images (Online publication - Provo, UT, USA: Ancestry.com Operations Inc, 2007.Original data - Various maritime reference sources. T715, Roll 1124. 28 Jul 1908. Kronprinzessin Cecilie, line 28.

BRUGUIER, OSCAR RICHARD

Source Title: **Burial record, Downs, Herbert E. and Viola**

http://www.findagrave.com/cgi-bin/fg.cgi?page=pv&GRid=97831269&PIpi=121866507

Citation: accessed 29 Nov 2015

BRUGUIER, VIOLA ELIZABETH BERTHA

DOWNS, HERBERT EUGENE

Source Title: **Red Bank Register**

Repository: Middletown Township Public Library and the Red Bank Public Library

Citation: Red Bank Register (, http://209.212.22.88/), Middletown Township Public Library and the Red Bank Public Library, Middletown Township Public Library, 55 New Monmouth Road, Middletown, NJ 07748, or Red Bank Public Library, 84 West Front Street, Red Bank, NJ 07701., Sep. 30, 1933, p.. http://209.212.22.88/data/rbr/1930-1939/1933/1933.09.20.pdf.

Bruguier, Charles Roy

Burke, Leonore Ada Bell

Source Title: **Social Security Death Index**

Repository: Ancestry.com

Citation: US, Social Security Death Index, 1935-Current; database, entries for individuals below:

Bruguier, Charles Roy. Died Feb 1969.

Bruguier, Edmund Francis. Died Jun 1983.

Bruguier, Francis A. Jr.. Died Jul 1962.

Bruguier, Paul O. Died 19 Mar 2001.

Bruguiere, Harold Oscar. Died Oct 1954.

Bruguiere, Oscar Robert. Died May 1982.

Bruguiere, Warren Kenneth. Died May 1980.

Field, Albert Everett. Died Aug 1984.

Hancox, Ernest Everland Jr. Died 24 Jul 1995.

Rogers, Geraldine Bruguier. Died 14 Apr 1994.

Steenburgh, Eugene Masten. Died Feb 1972.

Source Title: **U.S. Army, Register of Enlistments, 1798-1914**

Repository: Ancestry.com

Citation: Ancestry.com, U.S. Army, Register of Enlistments, 1798-1914 (Provo, UT, USA, Ancestry.com Operations Inc, 2007), Ancestry.com. 1854-1899, Hospital Stewards, p. 45, no. 757.

VON BRUGUIER, CARL ERNST AUGUST FRANCIS (Francois Bruguier)

Citation: Ancestry.com, U.S. Army, Register of Enlistments, 1798-1914 (Provo, UT, USA, Ancestry.com Operations Inc, 2007), Ancestry.com. 1859-1863, A-D, p. 103, line 1.

Citation: VON BRUGUIER, CARL ERNST AUGUST FRANCIS(Francois Bruguier)

Source Title: **U.S. Cemetery and Funeral Home Collection**

Repository: Ancestry.com

Citation: Ancestry.com, U.S. Cemetery and Funeral Home Collection (Provo, UT, USA, Ancestry.com Operations Inc, 2011), Ancestry.com. http://www.osceolamemgds.com/obituaries/George-Arthur-Bruguier-119347/; accessed 1 Dec 2015.

Bruguier, George Arthur

Source Title: **U.S. City Directories, 1821-1989**

Repository: Ancestry.com

Citation: Ancestry.com, U.S. City Directories, 1821-1989 (Provo, UT, USA, Ancestry.com Operations, Inc., 2011), Ancestry.com.

Bruguiere, Warren Kenneth

Citation: Ancestry.com, U.S. City Directories, 1821-1989 (Provo, UT, USA, Ancestry.com Operations, Inc., 2011), Ancestry.com.

KIRNER, JAMES JOSEPH

Citation: Ancestry.com, U.S. City Directories, 1821-1989 (Provo, UT, USA, Ancestry.com Operations, Inc., 2011), Ancestry.com.

DOWNS, SUZANNE BRUGUIER

Citation: Ancestry.com, U.S. City Directories, 1821-1989 (Provo, UT, USA, Ancestry.com Operations, Inc., 2011), Ancestry.com.

Bruguier, Wilhelmina Minerva

Citation: Ancestry.com, U.S. City Directories, 1821-1989 (Provo, UT, USA, Ancestry.com Operations, Inc., 2011), Ancestry.com.

BRUGUIER, VIOLA ELIZABETH BERTHA

Citation: Ancestry.com, U.S. City Directories, 1821-1989 (Provo, UT, USA, Ancestry.com Operations, Inc., 2011), Ancestry.com.

Bruguier, Helen T.

Citation: Ancestry.com, U.S. City Directories, 1821-1989 (Provo, UT, USA, Ancestry.com Operations, Inc., 2011), Ancestry.com.

Calver, Joseph H. Jr.

Citation: Ancestry.com, U.S. City Directories, 1821-1989 (Provo, UT, USA, Ancestry.com Operations, Inc., 2011), Ancestry.com.

Downs, Margaret Ruth

Citation: Ancestry.com, U.S. City Directories, 1821-1989 (Provo, UT, USA, Ancestry.com Operations, Inc., 2011), Ancestry.com.

Bruguiere, Warren Kenneth

Citation: Ancestry.com, U.S. City Directories, 1821-1989 (Provo, UT, USA, Ancestry.com Operations, Inc., 2011), Ancestry.com.

Bruguiere, Oscar Robert

Citation: Ancestry.com, U.S. City Directories, 1821-1989 (Provo, UT, USA, Ancestry.com Operations, Inc., 2011), Ancestry.com.

Reuther, Edna

Citation: Ancestry.com, U.S. City Directories, 1821-1989 (Provo, UT, USA, Ancestry.com Operations, Inc., 2011), Ancestry.com.

BRUGUIER, OSCAR RICHARD

Citation: Ancestry.com, U.S. City Directories, 1821-1989 (Provo, UT, USA, Ancestry.com Operations, Inc., 2011), Ancestry.com.

Bruguier, Dorothy Mae

Citation: Ancestry.com, U.S. City Directories, 1821-1989 (Provo, UT, USA, Ancestry.com Operations, Inc., 2011), Ancestry.com.

Bruguier, Dorothy Mae

Citation: Ancestry.com, U.S. City Directories, 1821-1989 (Provo, UT, USA, Ancestry.com Operations, Inc., 2011), Ancestry.com.

Heinzinger, Rudolph Fred

Citation: Ancestry.com, U.S. City Directories, 1821-1989 (Provo, UT, USA, Ancestry.com Operations, Inc., 2011), Ancestry.com.

Heinzinger, Rudolph Fred

Citation: Ancestry.com, U.S. City Directories, 1821-1989 (Provo, UT, USA, Ancestry.com Operations, Inc., 2011), Ancestry.com.

Bruguier, Dorothy Mae

Citation: Ancestry.com, U.S. City Directories, 1821-1989 (Provo, UT, USA, Ancestry.com Operations, Inc., 2011), Ancestry.com.

Heinzinger, Rudolph Fred

Citation: Ancestry.com, U.S. City Directories, 1821-1989 (Provo, UT, USA, Ancestry.com Operations, Inc., 2011), Ancestry.com.

DOWNS, SUZANNE BRUGUIER

Citation: Ancestry.com, U.S. City Directories, 1821-1989 (Provo, UT, USA, Ancestry.com Operations, Inc., 2011), Ancestry.com.

DOWNS, SUZANNE BRUGUIER

Citation: Ancestry.com, U.S. City Directories, 1821-1989 (Provo, UT, USA, Ancestry.com Operations, Inc., 2011), Ancestry.com.

DOWNS, HERBERT EUGENE

Citation: Ancestry.com, U.S. City Directories, 1821-1989 (Provo, UT, USA, Ancestry.com Operations, Inc., 2011), Ancestry.com.

DOWNS, HERBERT EUGENE

Citation: Ancestry.com, U.S. City Directories, 1821-1989 (Provo, UT, USA, Ancestry.com Operations, Inc., 2011), Ancestry.com.

BRUGUIER, VIOLA ELIZABETH BERTHA

Citation: Ancestry.com, U.S. City Directories, 1821-1989 (Provo, UT, USA, Ancestry.com Operations, Inc., 2011), Ancestry.com.

Downs, Margaret Ruth

Citation: Ancestry.com, U.S. City Directories, 1821-1989 (Provo, UT, USA, Ancestry.com Operations, Inc., 2011), Ancestry.com.

Bruguiere, Oscar Robert

Citation: Ancestry.com, U.S. City Directories, 1821-1989 (Provo, UT, USA, Ancestry.com Operations, Inc., 2011), Ancestry.com.

Bruguiere, Harold Oscar

Citation: Ancestry.com, U.S. City Directories, 1821-1989 (Provo, UT, USA, Ancestry.com Operations, Inc., 2011), Ancestry.com.

Smith, Altha Bunnell

Citation: Ancestry.com, U.S. City Directories, 1821-1989 (Provo, UT, USA, Ancestry.com Operations, Inc., 2011), Ancestry.com.

Bruguier, Alma Bertha

Source Title: **U.S. City Directories, 1821-1989 (con't)**

Repository: Ancestry.com

Citation: Ancestry.com, U.S. City Directories, 1821-1989 (Provo, UT, USA, Ancestry.com
Operations, Inc., 2011), Ancestry.com.

Rogers, Geraldine Bruguier

Citation: Ancestry.com, U.S. City Directories, 1821-1989 (Provo, UT, USA, Ancestry.com
Operations, Inc., 2011), Ancestry.com.

Rogers, Percival A. Steinmuller

Citation: Ancestry.com, U.S. City Directories, 1821-1989 (Provo, UT, USA, Ancestry.com
Operations, Inc., 2011), Ancestry.com.

Glover, John Henry III

Citation: Ancestry.com, U.S. City Directories, 1821-1989 (Provo, UT, USA, Ancestry.com
Operations, Inc., 2011), Ancestry.com.

Bruguiere, Warren Kenneth

Citation: Ancestry.com, U.S. City Directories, 1821-1989 (Provo, UT, USA, Ancestry.com
Operations, Inc., 2011), Ancestry.com.

Steenburgh, Eugene Masten

Citation: Ancestry.com, U.S. City Directories, 1821-1989 (Provo, UT, USA, Ancestry.com
Operations, Inc., 2011), Ancestry.com.

Reuther, Edna

Citation: Ancestry.com, U.S. City Directories, 1821-1989 (Provo, UT, USA, Ancestry.com
Operations, Inc., 2011), Ancestry.com.

Bruguier, Lillian Mary

Citation: Ancestry.com, U.S. City Directories, 1821-1989 (Provo, UT, USA, Ancestry.com
Operations, Inc., 2011), Ancestry.com.

FELDWEG, MARIE AUGUSTA

Citation: Ancestry.com, U.S. City Directories, 1821-1989 (Provo, UT, USA, Ancestry.com
Operations, Inc., 2011), Ancestry.com.

BRUGUIER, OSCAR RICHARD

Citation: Ancestry.com, U.S. City Directories, 1821-1989 (Provo, UT, USA, Ancestry.com
Operations, Inc., 2011), Ancestry.com.

DOWNS, HERBERT EUGENE

Source Title: **U.S. Passport Applications, 1795-1925**

Repository: Ancestry.com

Citation: Ancestry.com, U.S. Passport Applications, 1795-1925 (Provo, UT, USA, Ancestry.com
Operations, Inc., 2007), Ancestry.com, National Archives and Records Administration
(NARA); Washington D.C.; Passport Applications, January 2, 1906 - March 31, 1925;
Collection Number: ARC Identifier 583830 / MLR Number A1 534; NARA Series: M1490;
Roll #: 59, certificate no. 51196, 29 Apr 1908.

BRUGUIER, OSCAR RICHARD

Source Title: **U.S. World War II Army Enlistment Records, 1938-1946**

Repository: Ancestry.com

Citation: National Archives and Records Administration, U.S. World War II Army Enlistment
Records, 1938-1946 (Provo, UT, USA, Ancestry.com Operations Inc, 2005),
Ancestry.com. 27 Nov 1940. Newark, New Jersey.

Lish, Victor R

Source Title: **U.S., Civil War Pension Index: General Index to Pension Files, 1861-1934**

Repository: Ancestry.com

Citation: National Archives and Records Administration, U.S., Civil War Pension Index: General
Index to Pension Files, 1861-1934 (Provo, UT, USA, Ancestry.com Operations Inc,
2000), Ancestry.com. Roll T288_58. Browne, Charles-Brussard, Eugen; 20 Nov 1890; application no. 1011979.
VON BRUGUIER, CARL ERNST AUGUST FRANCIS

Source Title: U.S., Find A Grave Index, 1600s-Current

Repository: Ancestry.com

Citation: Ancestry.com, U.S., Find A Grave Index, 1600s-Current (Provo, UT, USA, Ancestry.com

Operations, Inc., 2012), Ancestry.com. 15 Oct 1994. Wall Church Cemetery, Monmouth Co., N.J.

Kirms, Albert

Citation: Ancestry.com, U.S., Find A Grave Index, 1600s-Current (Provo, UT, USA, Ancestry.com

Operations, Inc., 2012), Ancestry.com. 17 Apr 1960. Fred Hunter's Hollywood Memorial Gardens East, Broward Co.,
Florida.

Halloran, Patrick Joseph

Citation: Ancestry.com, U.S., Find A Grave Index, 1600s-Current (Provo, UT, USA, Ancestry.com

Operations, Inc., 2012), Ancestry.com. 30 Sep 2014. Jonesboro Cemetery, Nelson Co., Virginia.

Bruguiere, Thomas Harold

Citation: Ancestry.com, U.S., Find A Grave Index, 1600s-Current (Provo, UT, USA, Ancestry.com

Operations, Inc., 2012), Ancestry.com. (Edna Lish). 1956. Riverside Cemetery, Ocean Co., N.J.

Bruguier, Edna Mae

Citation: Ancestry.com, U.S., Find A Grave Index, 1600s-Current (Provo, UT, USA, Ancestry.com

Operations, Inc., 2012), Ancestry.com. (Helen Henderson). May 1978. North Hardyston Cemetery, Sussex Co., N.J.

Shauger, Helen

Citation: Ancestry.com, U.S., Find A Grave Index, 1600s-Current (Provo, UT, USA, Ancestry.com

Operations, Inc., 2012), Ancestry.com. 6 Jun 2010. North Hardyston Cemetery, Sussex Co., N.J.

Henderson, Kenneth M.

Citation: Ancestry.com, U.S., Find A Grave Index, 1600s-Current (Provo, UT, USA, Ancestry.com

Operations, Inc., 2012), Ancestry.com. 1960. North Hardyston Cemetery, Sussex Co., N.J.

Henderson, Francis

Citation: Ancestry.com, U.S., Find A Grave Index, 1600s-Current (Provo, UT, USA, Ancestry.com

Operations, Inc., 2012), Ancestry.com. 19 Jan 1985. North Hardyston Cemetery, Sussex Co., N.J.

Casterlin, Roy B.

Citation: Ancestry.com, U.S., Find A Grave Index, 1600s-Current (Provo, UT, USA, Ancestry.com

Operations, Inc., 2012), Ancestry.com. (Clara Casterlin). 13 Jul 1993. North Hardyston Cemetery, Sussex Co., N.J.

Henderson, Clara A.

Citation: Ancestry.com, U.S., Find A Grave Index, 1600s-Current (Provo, UT, USA, Ancestry.com

Operations, Inc., 2012), Ancestry.com. (Mary Bruguier). Jul 1942. Fair View Cemetery, Monmouth Co., N.J.

Boehm, Mary

Citation: Ancestry.com, U.S., Find A Grave Index, 1600s-Current (Provo, UT, USA, Ancestry.com

Operations, Inc., 2012), Ancestry.com. 1975. North Hardyston Cemetery, Sussex Co., N.J.

Henderson, Francis Bruguier

Citation: Ancestry.com, U.S., Find A Grave Index, 1600s-Current (Provo, UT, USA, Ancestry.com

Operations, Inc., 2012), Ancestry.com. 29 Dec 1961. Mount Olivet Cemetery, Monmouth Co., N.J.

Calver, Joseph H. Jr.

Citation: Ancestry.com, U.S., Find A Grave Index, 1600s-Current (Provo, UT, USA, Ancestry.com

Operations, Inc., 2012), Ancestry.com. 14 Jan 2014. Riverside National Cemetery, Riverside Co., California.

Calver, Gary

Citation: Ancestry.com, U.S., Find A Grave Index, 1600s-Current (Provo, UT, USA, Ancestry.com

Operations, Inc., 2012), Ancestry.com. 31 Oct 1947. North Hardyston Cemetery, Sussex Co., N.J.

Casterlin, Albert Havens

Citation: Ancestry.com, U.S., Find A Grave Index, 1600s-Current (Provo, UT, USA, Ancestry.com

Operations, Inc., 2012), Ancestry.com. 2 Apr 1982. First Presbyterian Churchyard, Monmouth Co., N.J.

DOWNS, HERBERT EUGENE

Citation: Ancestry.com, U.S., Find A Grave Index, 1600s-Current (Provo, UT, USA, Ancestry.com

Operations, Inc., 2012), Ancestry.com. (Francis Bruguier) 24 Dec 1906. Fairmount Cemetery, Essex Co., N.J.

VON BRUGUIER, CARL ERNST AUGUST FRANCIS

Citation: Ancestry.com, U.S., Find A Grave Index, 1600s-Current (Provo, UT, USA, Ancestry.com

Operations, Inc., 2012), Ancestry.com. 9 Oct 1950. Fairmount Cemetery, Essex Co., N.J.

BRUGUIER, OSCAR RICHARD

Citation: Ancestry.com, U.S., Find A Grave Index, 1600s-Current (Provo, UT, USA, Ancestry.com
Operations, Inc., 2012), Ancestry.com. (Minnie Bruguier Henderson) Mar 1977. North Hardyston Cemetery, Sussex
Co., N.J.

Bruguier, Minnie Pauline

Citation: Ancestry.com, U.S., Find A Grave Index, 1600s-Current (Provo, UT, USA, Ancestry.com

Operations, Inc., 2012), Ancestry.com. 20 May 1934. Fair View Cemetery, Monmouth Co., N.J.

Bruguier, Paul Charles

Citation: Ancestry.com, U.S., Find A Grave Index, 1600s-Current (Provo, UT, USA, Ancestry.com

Operations, Inc., 2012), Ancestry.com. 9 Jul 1962. Fair View Cemetery, Monmouth Co., N.J.

Bruguier, Francis A. Jr.

Citation: Ancestry.com, U.S., Find A Grave Index, 1600s-Current (Provo, UT, USA, Ancestry.com

Operations, Inc., 2012), Ancestry.com. 1972. Westhampton Memorial Park, Henrico Co., Virginia.

Steenburgh, Eugene Masten

Citation: Ancestry.com, U.S., Find A Grave Index, 1600s-Current (Provo, UT, USA, Ancestry.com

Operations, Inc., 2012), Ancestry.com. (Lillian Steenburgh). 1966. Westhampton Memorial Park, Henrico Co., Virginia.

Bruguier, Lillian Mary

Citation: Ancestry.com, U.S., Find A Grave Index, 1600s-Current (Provo, UT, USA, Ancestry.com

Operations, Inc., 2012), Ancestry.com. 13 Oct 2003. Saint Mary Cemetery, Worcester Co., Massachusetts

Bruguiere, Margot Mary

Citation: Ancestry.com, U.S., Find A Grave Index, 1600s-Current (Provo, UT, USA, Ancestry.com

Operations, Inc., 2012), Ancestry.com. 1984. Riverside Cemetery, Ocean County, N.J.

Lish, Victor R

Source Title: **U.S., Headstone Applications for Military Veterans, 1925-1963**

Repository: Ancestry.com

Citation: Ancestry.com, U.S., Headstone Applications for Military Veterans, 1925-1963 (Provo,
UT, USA, Ancestry.com Operations, Inc., 2012), Ancestry.com. 17 Apr 1960. Hollywood Memorial Gardens, Hollywood,
Florida.

Halloran, Patrick Joseph

Source Title: **U.S., Returns from Military Posts, 1806-1916**

Repository: Ancestry.com

Citation: Ancestry.com, U.S., Returns from Military Posts, 1806-1916 (Provo, UT, USA,
Ancestry.com Operations Inc, 2009), Ancestry.com, National Archives and Records
Administration (NARA); Washington, D.C.; Returns from U.S. Military Posts, 1800-1916;
Microfilm Serial: M617; Microfilm Roll: 443. New York, Ft. Hamilton, Sep 1864.

VON BRUGUIER, CARL ERNST AUGUST FRANCIS

Source Title: **U.S., Selected Quaker College Yearbooks and Alumni Directories, 1896-2003**

Repository: Ancestry.com

Citation: Ancestry.com, U.S., Selected Quaker College Yearbooks and Alumni Directories,
1896-2003 (Provo, UT, USA, Ancestry.com Operations, Inc., 2013), Ancestry.com.
Earlham College, Richmond, Indiana, 1967, p. 257.

Parker, Carl Hahn Jr.

Source Title: **U.S., Social Security Applications and Claims Index, 1936-2007**

Repository: Ancestry.com

Citation: Ancestry.com, U.S., Social Security Applications and Claims Index, 1936-2007 (Provo, UT, USA, Ancestry.com Operations, Inc., 2015), Ancestry.com. SSN 267-49-1201.

Bruguier, Lorraine D.

Citation: Ancestry.com, U.S., Social Security Applications and Claims Index, 1936-2007 (Provo, UT, USA, Ancestry.com Operations, Inc., 2015), Ancestry.com. 14 Nov 1923.

Rogers, Blair Oakley

Citation: Ancestry.com, U.S., Social Security Applications and Claims Index, 1936-2007 (Provo, UT, USA, Ancestry.com Operations, Inc., 2015), Ancestry.com. SSN 148-34-2313.

Bruguier, Eleanor Maybell

Citation: Ancestry.com, U.S., Social Security Applications and Claims Index, 1936-2007 (Provo, UT, USA, Ancestry.com Operations, Inc., 2015), Ancestry.com. SSN 150-20-0770.

Rogers, Geraldine Bruguier

Citation: Ancestry.com, U.S., Social Security Applications and Claims Index, 1936-2007 (Provo, UT, USA, Ancestry.com Operations, Inc., 2015), Ancestry.com. SSN 150-24-3358.

Calver, Joseph Henry

Citation: Ancestry.com, U.S., Social Security Applications and Claims Index, 1936-2007 (Provo, UT, USA, Ancestry.com Operations, Inc., 2015), Ancestry.com. SSN 143-24-2951.

Jennings, Jeanne Edna

Citation: Ancestry.com, U.S., Social Security Applications and Claims Index, 1936-2007 (Provo, UT, USA, Ancestry.com Operations, Inc., 2015), Ancestry.com. SSN 138-54-6647.

Bruguier, Alma Bertha

Citation: Ancestry.com, U.S., Social Security Applications and Claims Index, 1936-2007 (Provo, UT, USA, Ancestry.com Operations, Inc., 2015), Ancestry.com. SSN 137-05-8612.

BRUGUIER, OSCAR RICHARD

Citation: Ancestry.com, U.S., Social Security Applications and Claims Index, 1936-2007 (Provo, UT, USA, Ancestry.com Operations, Inc., 2015), Ancestry.com. (Dee Bruguier). SSN 146-20-9085.

Lennon, Dee

Citation: Ancestry.com, U.S., Social Security Applications and Claims Index, 1936-2007 (Provo, UT, USA, Ancestry.com Operations, Inc., 2015), Ancestry.com. SSN 141-24-0241.

Casterlin, Mahlon Roy

Citation: Ancestry.com, U.S., Social Security Applications and Claims Index, 1936-2007 (Provo, UT, USA, Ancestry.com Operations, Inc., 2015), Ancestry.com. (Beatrice H. Day). SSN 046-03-0984.

Henderson, Beatrice E.

Citation: Ancestry.com, U.S., Social Security Applications and Claims Index, 1936-2007 (Provo, UT, USA, Ancestry.com Operations, Inc., 2015), Ancestry.com. (Marie Toth). SSN 155-20-0927.

Henderson, Marie Audrey

Source Title: **U.S., Social Security Death Index, 1935-Current**

Repository: Ancestry.com

Citation: Ancestry.com, U.S., Social Security Death Index, 1935-Current (Provo, UT, USA, Ancestry.com Operations Inc, 2011), Ancestry.com, Number: 135-10-2085; Issue State: New Jersey; Issue Date: Before 1951.

Bruguiere, Oscar Robert

Citation: Ancestry.com, U.S., Social Security Death Index, 1935-Current (Provo, UT, USA, Ancestry.com Operations Inc, 2011), Ancestry.com, Number: 143-28-4657; Issue State: New Jersey; Issue Date: 1952-1954.

BRUGUIER, VIOLA ELIZABETH BERTHA

Citation: Ancestry.com, U.S., Social Security Death Index, 1935-Current (Provo, UT, USA, Ancestry.com Operations Inc, 2011), Ancestry.com, Issue State: New York; Issue Date: 1953-1955.

Field, Richard Douglas

Citation: Ancestry.com, U.S., Social Security Death Index, 1935-Current (Provo, UT, USA, Ancestry.com Operations Inc, 2011), Ancestry.com, Issue State: New York; Issue Date: Before 1951.

Field, Albert E.

Citation: Ancestry.com, U.S., Social Security Death Index, 1935-Current (Provo, UT, USA, Ancestry.com Operations Inc, 2011), Ancestry.com, Number: 002-16-4647; Issue State: New Hampshire; Issue Date: Before 1951.

Bruguiere, Harold Oscar

Citation: Ancestry.com, U.S., Social Security Death Index, 1935-Current (Provo, UT, USA, Ancestry.com Operations Inc, 2011), Ancestry.com, Number: 040-42-8987; Issue State: Connecticut; Issue Date: 1963-1964.

Bruguier, Minnie Pauline

Citation: Ancestry.com, U.S., Social Security Death Index, 1935-Current (Provo, UT, USA, Ancestry.com Operations Inc, 2011), Ancestry.com, Number: 120-07-7495; Issue State: New York; Issue Date: Before 1951.

Bruguiere, Warren Kenneth

Citation: Ancestry.com, U.S., Social Security Death Index, 1935-Current (Provo, UT, USA, Ancestry.com Operations Inc, 2011), Ancestry.com, Number: 135-01-5374; Issue State: New Jersey; Issue Date: Before 1951.

Hancox, Ernest Everland Jr.

Citation: Ancestry.com, U.S., Social Security Death Index, 1935-Current (Provo, UT, USA, Ancestry.com Operations Inc, 2011), Ancestry.com, Number: 135-03-3190; Issue State: New Jersey; Issue Date: Before 1951.

Bruguier, Laverne Audrey

Citation: Ancestry.com, U.S., Social Security Death Index, 1935-Current (Provo, UT, USA, Ancestry.com Operations Inc, 2011), Ancestry.com, Number: 135-12-7355; Issue State: New Jersey; Issue Date: Before 1951.

Henderson, Francis Bruguier

Citation: Ancestry.com, U.S., Social Security Death Index, 1935-Current (Provo, UT, USA, Ancestry.com Operations Inc, 2011), Ancestry.com, Number: 138-54-6647; Issue State: New Jersey; Issue Date: 1972.

Bruguier, Alma Bertha

Citation: Ancestry.com, U.S., Social Security Death Index, 1935-Current (Provo, UT, USA, Ancestry.com Operations Inc, 2011), Ancestry.com, Number: 145-07-3466; Issue State: New Jersey; Issue Date: Before 1951.

Bruguier, Wilhelmina Minerva

Citation: Ancestry.com, U.S., Social Security Death Index, 1935-Current (Provo, UT, USA, Ancestry.com Operations Inc, 2011), Ancestry.com, Number: 145-10-7643; Issue State: New Jersey; Issue Date: Before 1951.

Bruguier, Edmund Francis

Citation: Ancestry.com, U.S., Social Security Death Index, 1935-Current (Provo, UT, USA, Ancestry.com Operations Inc, 2011), Ancestry.com, Number: 146-20-9085; Issue State: New Jersey; Issue Date: Before 1951.

Lennon, Dee

Citation: Ancestry.com, U.S., Social Security Death Index, 1935-Current (Provo, UT, USA, Ancestry.com Operations Inc, 2011), Ancestry.com, Number: 147-01-6692; Issue State: New Jersey; Issue Date: Before 1951.

Bruguier, Francis A. Jr.

Citation: Ancestry.com, U.S., Social Security Death Index, 1935-Current (Provo, UT, USA, Ancestry.com Operations Inc, 2011), Ancestry.com, Number: 147-03-2829; Issue State: New Jersey; Issue Date: Before 1951.

Bruguier, Charles Roy

Citation: Ancestry.com, U.S., Social Security Death Index, 1935-Current (Provo, UT, USA, Ancestry.com Operations Inc, 2011), Ancestry.com, Number: 148-34-2313; Issue State: New Jersey; Issue Date: 1960-1961.

Bruguier, Eleanor Maybell

Citation: Ancestry.com, U.S., Social Security Death Index, 1935-Current (Provo, UT, USA, Ancestry.com Operations Inc, 2011), Ancestry.com, Number: 149-36-8093; Issue State: New Jersey; Issue Date: 1962.

Henderson, Iona W.

Citation: Ancestry.com, U.S., Social Security Death Index, 1935-Current (Provo, UT, USA, Ancestry.com Operations Inc, 2011), Ancestry.com, Number: 150-20-0770; Issue State: New Jersey; Issue Date: Before 1951.

Rogers, Geraldine Bruguier

Citation: Ancestry.com, U.S., Social Security Death Index, 1935-Current (Provo, UT, USA, Ancestry.com Operations Inc, 2011), Ancestry.com, Number: 150-22-0553; Issue State: New Jersey; Issue Date: Before 1951.

Steenburgh, Donald Rae

Citation: Ancestry.com, U.S., Social Security Death Index, 1935-Current (Provo, UT, USA, Ancestry.com Operations Inc, 2011), Ancestry.com, Number: 150-24-3358; Issue State: New Jersey; Issue Date: Before 1951.

Calver, Joseph Henry

Citation: Ancestry.com, U.S., Social Security Death Index, 1935-Current (Provo, UT, USA, Ancestry.com Operations Inc, 2011), Ancestry.com, Number: 155-20-0927; Issue State: New Jersey; Issue Date: Before 1951.

Henderson, Marie Audrey

Citation: Ancestry.com, U.S., Social Security Death Index, 1935-Current (Provo, UT, USA, Ancestry.com Operations Inc, 2011), Ancestry.com, Number: 204-24-3290; Issue State: Pennsylvania; Issue Date: Before 1951.

Parker, Carl Hahn Jr.

Citation: Ancestry.com, U.S., Social Security Death Index, 1935-Current (Provo, UT, USA, Ancestry.com Operations Inc, 2011), Ancestry.com, Number: 267-49-1201; Issue State: Florida; Issue Date: 1973.

Bruguier, Lorraine D.

Source Title: **U.S., World War I Draft Registration Cards, 1917-1918**

Repository: Ancestry.com

Citation: Ancestry.com, U.S., World War I Draft Registration Cards, 1917-1918 (Provo, UT, USA, Ancestry.com Operations Inc, 2005), Ancestry.com, Registration State: New Jersey; Registration County: Essex; Roll: 1753727; Draft Board: 4. SN 4184.

BRUGUIER, OSCAR RICHARD

Citation: Ancestry.com, U.S., World War I Draft Registration Cards, 1917-1918 (Provo, UT, USA, Ancestry.com Operations Inc, 2005), Ancestry.com, Registration State: New Jersey; Registration County: Essex; Roll: 1753733; Draft Board: 08. No. 1294.

Steenburgh, Eugene Masten

Citation: Ancestry.com, U.S., World War I Draft Registration Cards, 1917-1918 (Provo, UT, USA, Ancestry.com Operations Inc, 2005), Ancestry.com, Registration State: New Jersey; Registration County: Middlesex; Roll: 1712217; Draft Board: 2. No. 3297.

Bruguier, Francis A. Jr.

Citation: Ancestry.com, U.S., World War I Draft Registration Cards, 1917-1918 (Provo, UT, USA, Ancestry.com Operations Inc, 2005), Ancestry.com, Registration State: New Jersey; Registration County: Passaic; Roll: 1754427; Draft Board: 1. No. A3980.

Bruguier, Paul Charles

Citation: Ancestry.com, U.S., World War I Draft Registration Cards, 1917-1918 (Provo, UT, USA, Ancestry.com Operations Inc, 2005), Ancestry.com, Registration State: Ohio; Registration County: Columbiana; Roll: 1832017; Draft Board: 2. No. 135.

Halloran, Patrick Joseph

Source Title: **U.S., World War II Draft Registration Cards, 1942**

Repository: Ancestry.com

Citation: Ancestry.com, U.S., World War II Draft Registration Cards, 1942 (Provo, UT, USA, Ancestry.com Operations, Inc., 2010), Ancestry.com, National Archives and Records Administration (NARA); Washington, D.C.; State Headquarters: New Jersey. U738.

Steenburgh, Eugene Masten

Citation: Ancestry.com, U.S., World War II Draft Registration Cards, 1942 (Provo, UT, USA, Ancestry.com Operations, Inc., 2010), Ancestry.com, The National Archives at St. Louis; St. Louis, Missouri; World War II Draft Cards (Fourth Registration) for the State of New Jersey; State Headquarters: New Jersey; Microfilm Series: M1986. U3500.

Halloran, Patrick Joseph

Citation: Ancestry.com, U.S., World War II Draft Registration Cards, 1942 (Provo, UT, USA, Ancestry.com Operations, Inc., 2010), Ancestry.com, The National Archives at St. Louis; St. Louis, Missouri; World War II Draft Cards (Fourth Registration) for the State of New Jersey; State Headquarters: New Jersey; Microfilm Series: M1986. U1681.

Bruguier, Francis A. Jr.

Source Title: **United States Obituary Collection**

Repository: Ancestry.com

Citation: Ancestry.com, United States Obituary Collection (Provo, UT, USA, Ancestry.com Operations Inc, 2006), Ancestry.com, Newspaper: Manhasset Press; Publication Date: 20 08 2010; Publication Place: Manhasset, NY, USA. http://www.antonnews.com/manhassetpress/obits/9880-obituary-dr-richard-field.html

Field, Richard Douglas

Citation: Ancestry.com, United States Obituary Collection (Provo, UT, USA, Ancestry.com Operations Inc, 2006), Ancestry.com, Newspaper: The Reporter-Herald; Publication Date: 16 06 2010; Publication Place: Loveland, CO, USA.

Henderson, Kenneth M.

Citation: Ancestry.com, United States Obituary Collection (Provo, UT, USA, Ancestry.com Operations Inc, 2006), Ancestry.com, Publication Date: 14 Feb 2012; Publication Place: Lancaster, Pennsylvania, USA. (Joyce Diane Downs Parker). http://lancasteronline.com/obituaries/joyce-diane-downs-parker/article_29d8627b-a583-56b2-b778-d9162d47e0d8.html (accessed 8 Dec 2015).

Downs, Joyce Diane

Citation: Ancestry.com, United States Obituary Collection (Provo, UT, USA, Ancestry.com Operations Inc, 2006), Ancestry.com, Publication Date: 21 Nov 2014; Publication Place: Lynchburg, Virginia, USA. http://www.newsadvance.com/obituaries/bruguiere-thomas-harold/article_936dfb14-3c08-580d-a738-a08c01c5c949.html (accessed 8 Dec 2015).

Bruguiere, Thomas Harold

Citation: Ancestry.com, United States Obituary Collection (Provo, UT, USA, Ancestry.com Operations Inc, 2006), Ancestry.com, Publication Date: 26 Jan 2014; Publication Place: Irvine, California, USA. http://obits.ocregister.com/obituaries/orangecounty/obituary.aspx?n=gary-richard-calver&&pid=169344498 (accessed 9 Dec 2015).

Calver, Gary

Citation: Ancestry.com, United States Obituary Collection (Provo, UT, USA, Ancestry.com Operations Inc, 2006), Ancestry.com, Publication Date: 5 Aug 2012; Publication Place: Newton, New Jersey, USA. http://www.legacy.com/obituaries/njherald/obituary.aspx?n=reginald-dean-casterlin-nov----aug--&pid=158976647 .(accessed 9 Dec 2015).

Casterlin, Reginald Dean

Source Title: **US, Register of Civil, Military, and Naval Service, 1863-1959**

Repository: Ancestry.com

Citation: Ancestry.com, US, Register of Civil, Military, and Naval Service, 1863-1959 (Provo, UT, USA, Ancestry.com Operations, Inc., 2014), Ancestry.com. 1905, Vol. 2, p. 560.

VON BRUGUIER, CARL ERNST AUGUST FRANCIS

Source Title: **Virginia, Death Records, 1912-2014**

Repository: Ancestry.com

Citation: Ancestry.com, Virginia, Death Records, 1912-2014 (Provo, UT, USA, Ancestry.com Operations, Inc., 2015), Ancestry.com. (Lillian Steenburgh) 1966. SFN 66 014931.

Bruguier, Lillian Mary

Citation: Ancestry.com, Virginia, Death Records, 1912-2014 (Provo, UT, USA, Ancestry.com Operations, Inc., 2015), Ancestry.com. 1972. SFN 72 004942.

Steenburgh, Eugene Masten

Citation: Ancestry.com, Virginia, Death Records, 1912-2014 (Provo, UT, USA, Ancestry.com Operations, Inc., 2015), Ancestry.com. 13 Oct 2001. Hanover, Virginia.

Steenburgh, Donald Rae

Citation: Ancestry.com, Virginia, Death Records, 1912-2014 (Provo, UT, USA, Ancestry.com Operations, Inc., 2015), Ancestry.com. (Lorraine Rauch).

Bruguier, Lorraine D. 24 Jan 2003. Spotsylvania, Virginia.

Source Title: **Virginia, Marriage Records, 1936-2014**

Repository: Ancestry.com

Citation: Ancestry.com, Virginia, Marriage Records, 1936-2014 (Provo, UT, USA, Ancestry.com Operations, Inc., 2015), Ancestry.com. 1968. SFN 68 040201.

Steenburgh, Eugene Masten

Citation: Ancestry.com, Virginia, Marriage Records, 1936-2014 (Provo, UT, USA, Ancestry.com Operations, Inc., 2015), Ancestry.com. 1955. SFN 02948.

Steenburgh, Donald Rae

Sutphin, Lila

Citation: Ancestry.com, Virginia, Marriage Records, 1936-2014 (Provo, UT, USA, Ancestry.com Operations, Inc., 2015), Ancestry.com. 1952 SFN 16985.

Bruguiere, Thomas Harold

Citation: Dickie, Emilie Louise

Source Title: Web: New Jersey, Find A Grave Index, 1664-2012

   Repository: Ancestry.com

      Citation: Ancestry.com, Web: New Jersey, Find A Grave Index, 1664-2012 (Provo, UT, USA, Ancestry.com Operations, Inc., 2012),
            Ancestry.com. (Edna M. Lish). Toms River, Ocean County, N.J.
            Bruguier, Edna Mae

Source Title: Web: Obituary Daily Times Index, 1995-Current

   Repository: Ancestry.com

      Citation: Ancestry.com, Web: Obituary Daily Times Index, 1995-Current (Provo, UT, USA, Ancestry.com Operations, Inc., 2012),
            Ancestry.com. 19 Sep 2000.

BRUGUIER, VIOLA ELIZABETH BERTHA

INDEX-Note: Women are indexed by maiden name, with married name in parentheses.

Made in the USA
Middletown, DE
08 February 2020

84406889R00071